LibGDX Game Development By Example

Learn how to create your very own game using the LibGDX cross-platform framework

James Cook

BIRMINGHAM - MUMBAI

LibGDX Game Development By Example

First published: August 2015

Production reference: 1210815

Published by Packt Publishing Ltd.
Livery Place
35 Livery Street
Birmingham B3 2PB, UK.

ISBN 978-1-78528-144-0

www.packtpub.com

Credits

Author
James Cook

Reviewers
Pavel Czempin
Lévêque Michel
Sudarshan Shetty

Acquisition Editors
Subho Gupta
James Jones

Content Development Editor
Nikhil Potdukhe

Technical Editor
Abhishek R. Kotian

Copy Editor
Pranjali Chury

Project Coordinator
Mary Alex

Proofreader
Safis Editing

Indexer
Monica Ajmera Mehta

Graphics
Dan Smallman
Jason Monteiro

Production Coordinator
Arvindkumar Gupta

Cover Work
Arvindkumar Gupta

About the Author

James Cook is a Java software developer from London, England. He is currently touring Australia. He has developed software ranging from banking and mobile applications to games. He has worked for large gaming companies, such as Electronic Arts, Playfish, and Plumbee.

During the day, he can be found working on rapid application prototyping for new social casino experiences. However, during the night, he collaborates with his longtime working partner, Dan Smallman, for Super Cookie Games to create games such as Super Bomb Noms, OMG Dancer!, and Betamax—Sherbet Plains.

Super Cookie Games started out as a simple endeavor for James and Dan to learn how to make games and deliver them to Android, iOS, and the Web. Choosing LibGDX as the platform was a key component for the success of this duo, with six different games across three app stores culminating in 50,000 downloads—a testament to LibGDX and its brilliant feature set and ability.

I would like to thank Dan because our teamwork over the last 4 years and our continuous efforts to try out new things while making games led me to write this book. I would like to thank Barry Cranford, who first put me in touch with Dan many years ago. I would also like to thank James Jones and Nikhil Potdukhe at Packt Publishing; without them, this book would not have been possible.

About the Reviewers

Pavel Czempin is currently completing an internship in the software field and plans to study engineering at a German university. Most of his programming experience stems from his early enrollment in a bachelor's course in computer science. In his free time, he likes to program and develop games.

You can find some of his projects on his GitHub page at https://github.com/Valep42.

Lévêque Michel has a bachelor's degree in information technology. He worked as a Java developer for 8 years and is currently working on a LibGDX point-and-click game as a core programmer.

> I would like to thank the author of this book and the team at Packt Publishing for giving me the opportunity to review this great book.

Sudarshan Shetty is a software developer who builds mobile apps for the order management system. He uses LibGDX to build BI dashboards and data visualization software. When not programming, he engages in gardening as a hobby with his wife, Anuradha, and kids, Shameen and Shamika.

www.PacktPub.com

Support files, eBooks, discount offers, and more

For support files and downloads related to your book, please visit www.PacktPub.com.

Did you know that Packt offers eBook versions of every book published, with PDF and ePub files available? You can upgrade to the eBook version at www.PacktPub.com and as a print book customer, you are entitled to a discount on the eBook copy. Get in touch with us at service@packtpub.com for more details.

At www.PacktPub.com, you can also read a collection of free technical articles, sign up for a range of free newsletters and receive exclusive discounts and offers on Packt books and eBooks.

https://www2.packtpub.com/books/subscription/packtlib

Do you need instant solutions to your IT questions? PacktLib is Packt's online digital book library. Here, you can search, access, and read Packt's entire library of books.

Why subscribe?

- Fully searchable across every book published by Packt
- Copy and paste, print, and bookmark content
- On demand and accessible via a web browser

Free access for Packt account holders

If you have an account with Packt at www.PacktPub.com, you can use this to access PacktLib today and view 9 entirely free books. Simply use your login credentials for immediate access.

Table of Contents

Preface

Video games have been around for over 30 years now and many of us have grown up with some form of experience playing video games. Most of us will want to go on and make our own games. It has never been easier to create your own game and deliver it to the world, whether you want to make a game to share with your friends or want to start a career in the game development industry.

Owing to the ease of development, a whole host of different tools are available to help you create games. Depending on whether you want to develop for desktop, iOS, Android, or HTML5, there are different tools available. However, what if you wanted to develop for all platforms? This is where an awesome framework called LibGDX comes in.

If you are reading this book, you are probably already aware of LibGDX. You may not be proficient in it, and you may not even have used it yet. But that's OK! That's why you are reading this book. We will use LibGDX to create a series of games, each game introducing another set of features of LibGDX. Hopefully, by the end of this book, you will have the foundation to go on and comfortably start making your own games.

What this book covers

Chapter 1, *Getting to Know LibGDX*, introduces us to LibGDX and helps us to set up our development environment to get ready to create our first ever LibGDX project.

Chapter 2, *Let's Get These Snakes Out of This Book!*, covers creating our first game using LibGDX—Snake! This also covers the game cycle and how to handle input through LibGDX.

Chapter 3, Making That Snake Slick, covers creating game states, continuing with our Snake game from the previous chapter. This also covers an introduction to the techniques used to help with development and talks about handling different screen sizes and resolutions.

Chapter 4, What the Flap Is the Hype About?, explains how to create our second game, Flappy Bee, our own interpretation of a famous mobile game. Here, we are introduced to handling animations and using LibGDX's Scene2D to create a GUI menu.

Chapter 5, Making Your Bird More Flightworthy, explores our Flappy Bee game a little further, where we look at handling assets in LibGDX as well as using one of the tools—Heiro—for converting fonts.

Chapter 6, Onto the Next Platform...Game, introduces you to our next game, where we create a simple platform game—Pete the Squirrel! Here, we cover the use of a tile mapping tool—Tiled—and discuss how LibGDX integrates with it.

Chapter 7, Extending the Platform, discusses handling the LibGDX camera to create scrolling levels and introduces playing sounds.

Chapter 8, Why Are All the Birds Angry?, covers our final game in this book. We look at creating our own version of Angry Birds, where we look at how LibGDX and Box2D work together to create an awesome game.

Chapter 9, Even Angrier Birds!, closes our final game by looking at object pooling in LibGDX and showing how it can be used to help with performance and memory management.

Chapter 10, Exporting Our Games to the Platforms, introduces you to how we can use LibGDX to export our awesome games to Android, iOS, and HTML5.

Chapter 11, Third-party Services, covers integrating a platform-specific service into a LibGDX game.

What you need for this book

It is entirely possible to enjoy and learn from this book without having to use a computer. However, I would recommend that you run the examples while you read this book.

The first chapter covers how to get your computer set up to run these examples. A computer with a minimum of a dual core processor and 4GB RAM is preferable.

Who this book is for

This book is about getting started with making games using LibGDX. So, complete beginners are more than welcome on our journey to create games. No previous experience of LibGDX is necessary, however, some basic Java knowledge will help.

Conventions

In this book, you will find a number of text styles that distinguish between different kinds of information. Here are some examples of these styles and an explanation of their meaning.

Code words in text, database table names, folder names, filenames, file extensions, pathnames, dummy URLs, user input, and Twitter handles are shown as follows: "The Gdx.log() methods is extremely handy when it comes to debugging our games"

A block of code is set as follows:

```
public void render(float delta) {
    batch.begin();
    sprite.draw(batch);
    batch.end();
}
```

Any command-line input or output is written as follows:

```
java -verlsion
```

New terms and **important words** are shown in bold. Words that you see on the screen, for example, in menus or dialog boxes, appear in the text like this: "Before we hit the **Generate** button, let's just take a look at what we are creating."

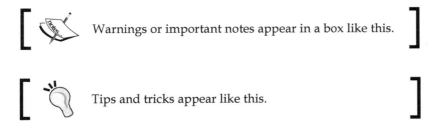

Warnings or important notes appear in a box like this.

Tips and tricks appear like this.

Reader feedback

Feedback from our readers is always welcome. Let us know what you think about this book—what you liked or disliked. Reader feedback is important for us as it helps us develop titles that you will really get the most out of.

To send us general feedback, simply e-mail feedback@packtpub.com, and mention the book's title in the subject of your message.

If there is a topic that you have expertise in and you are interested in either writing or contributing to a book, see our author guide at www.packtpub.com/authors.

Customer support

Now that you are the proud owner of a Packt book, we have a number of things to help you to get the most from your purchase.

Downloading the example code

You can download the example code files from your account at http://www.packtpub.com for all the Packt Publishing books you have purchased. If you purchased this book elsewhere, you can visit http://www.packtpub.com/support and register to have the files e-mailed directly to you.

Downloading the color images of this book

We also provide you with a PDF file that has color images of the screenshots/diagrams used in this book. The color images will help you better understand the changes in the output. You can download this file from https://www.packtpub.com/sites/default/files/downloads/B04176_1440OS_ColorImages.pdf.

Errata

Although we have taken every care to ensure the accuracy of our content, mistakes do happen. If you find a mistake in one of our books—maybe a mistake in the text or the code—we would be grateful if you could report this to us. By doing so, you can save other readers from frustration and help us improve subsequent versions of this book. If you find any errata, please report them by visiting http://www.packtpub.com/submit-errata, selecting your book, clicking on the **Errata Submission Form** link, and entering the details of your errata. Once your errata are verified, your submission will be accepted and the errata will be uploaded to our website or added to any list of existing errata under the Errata section of that title.

To view the previously submitted errata, go to https://www.packtpub.com/books/content/support and enter the name of the book in the search field. The required information will appear under the **Errata** section.

Piracy

Piracy of copyrighted material on the Internet is an ongoing problem across all media. At Packt, we take the protection of our copyright and licenses very seriously. If you come across any illegal copies of our works in any form on the Internet, please provide us with the location address or website name immediately so that we can pursue a remedy.

Please contact us at copyright@packtpub.com with a link to the suspected pirated material.

We appreciate your help in protecting our authors and our ability to bring you valuable content.

Questions

If you have a problem with any aspect of this book, you can contact us at questions@packtpub.com, and we will do our best to address the problem.

1
Getting to Know LibGDX

Creating games is fun, and that is why I like to do it. The process of having an idea for a game to actually delivering it has changed over the years. Back in the 1980s, it was quite common that the top games around were created by either a single person or a very small team. However, anyone who is lucky enough (in my opinion) to see games grow from being quite a simplistic affair to the complex beast that the now AAA titles are, must have also seen the resources needed for these grow with them. The advent of mobile gaming reduced the barrier for entry; once again, the smaller teams could produce a game that could be a worldwide hit! Now, there are games of all genres and complexities available across major gaming platforms.

Due to this explosion in the number of games being made, new general-purpose game-making tools appeared in the community. Previously, the in-house teams built and maintained very specific game engines for their games; however, this would have led to a lot of reinventing the wheel. I hate to think how much time I would have lost if for each of my games, I had to start from scratch.

Now, instead of worrying about how to display a 2D image on the screen, I can focus on creating that fun player experience I have in my head. My tool of choice? **LibGDX**.

Introducing LibGDX

Before I dive into what LibGDX is, here is how LibGDX describes itself. From the LibGDX wiki — `https://github.com/libgdx/libgdx/wiki/Introduction`:

> *LibGDX is a cross-platform game and visualization development framework.*

So what does that actually mean? What can LibGDX do for us game-makers that allows us to focus purely on the gameplay?

To begin with, LibGDX is Java-based. This means you can reuse a lot, and I mean a lot, of tools that already exist in the Java world.

I can imagine a few of you right now must be thinking, "But Java? For a game? I thought Java is supposed to be slow". To a certain extent, this can be true; after all, Java is still an interpreted language that runs in a virtual machine. However, to combat the need for the best possible performance, LibGDX takes advantage of the **Java Native Interface (JNI)** to implement native platform code and negate the performance disadvantage. One of the beauties of LibGDX is that it allows you to go as low-level as you would like. Direct access to filesystems, input devices, audio devices, and OpenGL (via OpenGL ES 2.0/3.0) is provided. However, the added edge LibGDX gives is that with the APIs that are built on top of these low-level facilities, displaying an image on the screen takes now a days only a few lines of code.

 A full list of the available features for LibGDX can be found here: http://libgdx.badlogicgames.com/features.html

I am happy to wait here while you go and check it out.

Impressive list of features, no?

So, how cross-platform is this gaming platform? This is probably what you are thinking now. Well, as mentioned before, games are being delivered on many different platforms, be it consoles, PCs, or mobiles.

LibGDX currently supports the following platforms:

- Windows
- Linux
- Mac OS X
- Android
- BlackBerry
- iOS
- HTML/WebGL

That is a pretty comprehensive list. Being able to write your game once and have it delivered to all the preceding platforms is pretty powerful.

At this point, I would like to mention that LibGDX is completely free and open source. You can go to https://github.com/libGDX/libGDX and check out all the code in all its glory. If the code does something and you would like to understand how, it is all possible; or, if you find a bug, you can make a fix and offer it back to the community.

Along with the source code, there are plenty of tests and demos showcasing what LibGDX can do, and more importantly, how to do it. Check out the wiki for more information:

- `https://github.com/libgdx/libgdx/wiki/Running-Demos`
- `https://github.com/libgdx/libgdx/wiki/Running-Tests`

"Who else uses LibGDX?" is quite a common query that comes up during a LibGDX discussion. Well it turns out just about everyone has used it. Google released a game called *"Ingress"* (`https://play.google.com/store/apps/details?id=com.nianticproject.ingress&hl=en`) on the play store in 2013, which uses LibGDX. Even Intel (`https://software.intel.com/en-us/articles/getting-started-with-libgdx-a-cross-platform-game-development-framework`) has shown an interest in LibGDX. Finally, I would like to end this section with another quote from the LibGDX website:

> *LibGDX aims to be a framework rather than an engine, acknowledging that there is no one-size-fits-all solution. Instead we give you powerful abstractions that let you chose how you want to write your game or application.*
>
> *LibGDX wiki* — `https://github.com/libgdx/libgdx/wiki/Introduction`

This means that you can use the available tools if you want to; if not, you can dive deeper into the framework and create your own!

Setting up LibGDX

We know by now that LibGDX is this awesome tool for creating games across many platforms with the ability to iterate on our code at superfast speeds. But how do we start using it?

Thankfully, some helpful people have made the setup process quite easy. However, before we get to that part, we need to ensure that we have the prerequisites installed, which are as follows:

- Java Development Kit 7+ (at the time of writing, version 8 is available)
- Android SDK

Not that big a list! Follow the given steps:

1. First things first. Go to `http://www.oracle.com/technetwork/java/javase/downloads/index.html`.

2. Download and install the latest JDK if you haven't already done so. Oracle developers are wonderful people and have provided a useful installation guide, which you can refer to if you are unsure on how to install the JDK, at

   `http://docs.oracle.com/javase/8/docs/technotes/guides/install/`
   `install_overview.html`.

3. Once you have installed the JDK, open up the command line and run the following command:

   `java -version`

   If it is installed correctly, you should get an output similar to this:

   ```
   >java -version
   java version "1.8.0_51"
   Java(TM) SE Runtime Environment (build 1.8.0_51-b16)
   Java HotSpot(TM) 64-Bit Server VM (build 25.51-b03, mixed mode)
   >
   ```

4. If you generate an error while doing this, consult the Oracle installation documentation and try again.

5. One final touch would be to ensure that we have JAVA_HOME configured. On the command line, perform the following:

   ° For Windows, set JAVA_HOME = `C:\Path\ToJDK\`

   ° For Linux and Mac OSX, export JAVA_HOME = `/Path/ToJDK/`

6. Next, on to the Android SDK.

At the time of writing, **Android Studio** has just been released. Android Studio is an IDE offered by Google that is built upon **JetBrains IntelliJ IDEA Java IDE**. If you feel comfortable using Android Studio as your IDE, and as a developer who has used IntelliJ for the last 5 years, I suggest that you at least give it a go. You can download Android Studio + Android SDK in a bundle from here:

`http://developer.android.com/sdk/index.html`

Alternatively, if you plan to use a different IDE (**Eclipse** or **NetBeans**, for example) you can just install the tools from the following URL:

`http://developer.android.com/sdk/index.html#Other`

You can find the installation instructions here:

`https://developer.android.com/sdk/installing/index.html?pkg=tools`

However, I would like to point out that the official IDE for Android is now Android Studio and no longer Eclipse with ADT.

For the sake of simplicity, we will only focus on making games for desktops for the greater part of this book. We will look at exporting to Android and iOS later on.

Once the Android SDK is installed, it would be well worth running the SDK manager application; so, finalize the set up.

If you opt to use Android Studio, you can access this from the SDK Manager icon in the toolbar. Alternatively, you can also access it as follows:

- **On Windows**: Double-click on the SDK's `Manager.exe` file at the root of the Android SDK directory
- **On Mac/Linux**: Open a terminal and navigate to the `tools/` directory in the location where the Android SDK is installed, then execute Android SDK.

The following screen might appear:

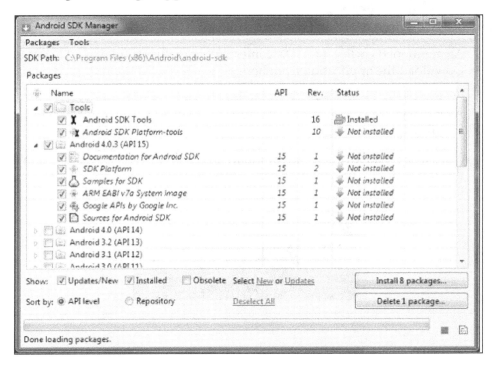

As a minimum configuration, select:

- **Android SDK Tools**
- **Android SDK Platform-tools**
- **Android SDK Build-tools** (latest available version)
- Latest version of **SDK Platform**

Let them download and install the selected configuration. Then that's it!

Well, not really. We just need to set the `ANDROID_HOME` environment variable. To do this, we can open up a command line and run the following command:

- **On Windows**: Set `ANDROID_HOME=C:/Path/To/Your/Android/Sdk`
- **On Linux** and **Mac OS X**: Export `ANDROID_HOME=/Path/To/Your/Android/Sdk`

Phew! With that done, we can now move on to the best part—creating our first ever LibGDX game!

Creating a project

Follow the given steps to create your own project:

1. As mentioned earlier, LibGDX comes with a really useful project setup tool. Download the application from here:

   `http://libgdx.badlogicgames.com/download.html`

   At the time of writing, it is the big red "**Download Setup App**" button in the middle of your screen.

2. Once downloaded, open the command line and navigate to the location of the application. You will notice that it is a JAR file type. This means we need to use Java to run it.

3. Running this will open the setup UI:

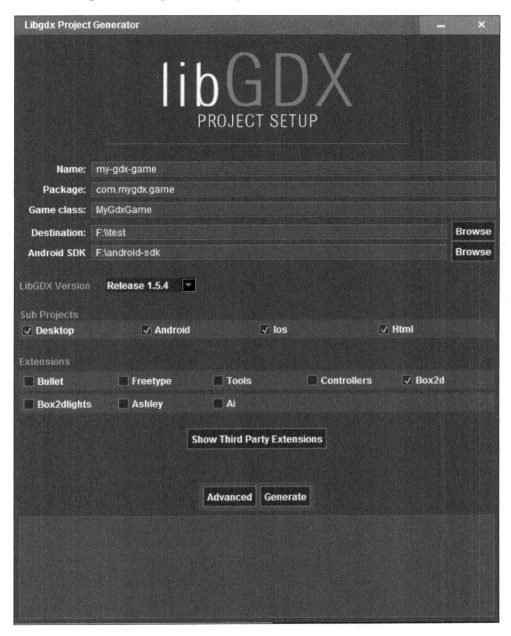

Before we hit the **Generate** button, let's just take a look at what we are creating here:

- **Name**: This is the name of our game.
- **Package**: This is the Java package our game code will be developed in.
- **Game class**: This parameter sets the name of our game class, where the magic happens!
- **Destination**: This is the project's directory. You can change this to any location of your choice.
- **Android SDK**: This is the location of the SDK. If this isn't set correctly, we can change it here. Going forward, it might be worth setting the ANDROID_ HOME environment variable.

Next is the version of LibGDX we want to use. At time of writing, the version is 1.5.4.

Now, let's move on to the subprojects. As we are only interested in desktops at the moment, let's deselect the others.

Finally, we come to extensions. Feel free to uncheck any that are checked. We won't be needing any of them at this point in time. For more information on available extensions, check out the LibGDX wiki (https://github.com/libgdx/libgdx/wiki).

Once all is set, let's hit the **Generate** button!

There is a little window at the bottom of the UI that will now spring to life. Here, it will show you the setup progress as it downloads the necessary setup files.

Once complete, open that command line, navigate to the directory, and run your preferred tree command (in Windows, it is just "tree").

Hopefully, you will have the same directory layout as the previous image shows.

The astute among you will now ask, "What is this Gradle?" and quite rightly so. I haven't mentioned it yet, although it appears twice in our projects directory.

What is Gradle?

Well, **Gradle** is a very excellent build tool and LibGDX leverages its abilities to look after the dependencies, build process, and IDE integration. This is especially useful if you are going to be working in a team with a shared code base. Even if you are not, the dependency management aspect is worth it alone.

Anyone who isn't familiar with dependency management may well be used to downloading Java JARs manually and placing them in a `libs` folder, but they might run into problems later when the JAR they just downloaded needs another JAR, and so on. The dependency management will take care of this for you and even better is that the LibGDX setup application takes care of this for you by already describing the dependencies that you need to run!

Within LibGDX, there is something called the **Gradle Wrapper**. This is essentially the Gradle application embedded into the project. This allows portability of our project, as now if we want someone else to run it, they can.

I guess this leads us to the question, how do we use Gradle to run our project? In the LibGDX wiki (`https://github.com/libgdx/libgdx/wiki/Gradle-on-the-Commandline`), you will find a comprehensive list of commands that can be used while developing your game.

However, for now, we will only cover the desktop project.

What you may not have noticed is that the setup application actually generates a very simple "Hello World" game for us. So, we have something we can run from the command line right away!

Let's go for it!

On our command line, let's run the following:

- On Windows: `gradlew desktop:run`

- On Linux and Mac OS X: `./gradlew desktop:run`

The following screen will appear once you execute the preceding command:

```
>gradlew desktop:run
Starting a new Gradle Daemon for this build (subsequent builds will be faster).
Configuration on demand is an incubating feature.
:core:compileJava
warning: [options] bootstrap class path not set in conjunction with -source 1.6
1 warning
:core:processResources UP-TO-DATE
:core:classes
:core:jar
:desktop:compileJava
warning: [options] bootstrap class path not set in conjunction with -source 1.6
1 warning
:desktop:processResources UP-TO-DATE
:desktop:classes
> Building 87% > :desktop:run
```

You will get an output similar to the preceding screenshot. Don't worry if it suddenly wants to start downloading the dependencies. This is our dependency management in action! All those JARs and native binaries are being downloaded and put on to classpaths. But, we don't care. We are here to create games!

So, after the command prompt has finished downloading the files, it should then launch the "Hello World" game.

Awesome! You have just launched your very first LibGDX game!

Although, before we get too excited, you will notice that not much actually happens here. It is just a red screen with the **Bad Logic Games** logo.

I think now is the time to look at the code!

Importing a project

So far, we have launched the "Hello World" game via the command line, and haven't seen a single line of code so far. Let's change that.

To do this, I will use IntelliJ IDEA. If you are using Android Studio, the screenshots will look familiar. If you are using Eclipse, I am sure you will be able to see the common concepts.

To begin with, we need to generate the appropriate IDE project files. Again, this is using Gradle to do the heavy lifting for us.

Once again, on the command line, run the following (pick the one that applies):

- **On Windows:** `gradlew idea` or `gradlew eclipse`
- **On Linux and Mac OS X:** `./gradlew idea` or `./gradlew eclipse`

Now, Gradle will have generated some project files. Open your IDE of choice and open the project.

> If you require more help, check out the following wiki pages:
> - `https://github.com/libgdx/libgdx/wiki/Gradle-and-Eclipse`
> - `https://github.com/libgdx/libgdx/wiki/Gradle-and-Intellij-IDEA`
> - `https://github.com/libgdx/libgdx/wiki/Gradle-and-NetBeans`

Once the project is open, have a poke around and look at some of the files. I think our first port of call should be the `build.gradle` file in the root of the project. Here, you will see that the layout of our project is defined and the dependencies we require are on display.

It is a good time to mention that going forward, there will be new releases of LibGDX, and to update our project to the latest version, all we need to do is update the following property:

```
gdxVersion = '1.6.4'
```

Now, run your game and Gradle will kick in and download everything for you!

Next, we should look for our game class, remember the one we specified in the setup application—MyGdxGame.java? Find it, open it, and be in awe of how simple it is to display that red screen and Bad Logic Games logo. In fact, I am going to paste the code here for you to see how simple it is:

```java
public class MyGdxGame extends ApplicationAdapter {
  SpriteBatch batch;
  Texture img;
  @Override
  public void create () {
    batch = new SpriteBatch();
    img = new Texture("badlogic.jpg");
  }

  @Override
  public void render () {
    Gdx.gl.glClearColor(1, 0, 0, 1);
    Gdx.gl.glClear(GL20.GL_COLOR_BUFFER_BIT);
    batch.begin();
    batch.draw(img, 0, 0);
    batch.end();
  }
}
```

We will cover what all this means in the next chapter, but, essentially, we can see that when the create() method is called, it sets up a SpriteBatch batch and creates a texture from a given JPEG file. Then, on the render() method, this is called on every iteration of the game loop; it covers the screen with the color red, then it draws the texture at the (0, 0) coordinate location.

Finally, we will look at the `DesktopLauncher` class, which is responsible for running the game in the desktop environment. Let's take a look at the following code snippet:

```
public class DesktopLauncher {
  public static void main (String[] arg) {
    LwjglApplicationConfiguration config = new
    LwjglApplicationConfiguration();
    new LwjglApplication(new MyGdxGame(), config);
  }
}
```

The preceding code shows how simple it is. We have a configuration object that will define how our desktop application runs, setting things like screen resolution and framerate, amongst others. In fact, this is an excellent time to utilize the open source aspect of LibGDX. In your IDE, click through to the `LwjglApplicationConfiguration` class. You will see all the properties that can be tweaked and notes on what they mean.

The instance of the `LwjglApplicationConfiguration` class is then passed to the constructor of another class `LwjglApplication`, along with an instance of our `MyGdxGame` class.

Finally, those who have worked with Java a lot in the past will recognize that it is wrapped in a main method—a traditional entry point for a Java application.

That is all that is needed to create and launch a desktop-only LibGDX game.

Downloading the example code

You can download the example code files from your account at http://www.packtpub.com for all the Packt Publishing books you have purchased. If you purchased this book elsewhere, you can visit http://www.packtpub.com/support and register to have the files e-mailed directly to you.

Summary

In this chapter, we looked at what LibGDX is about and how to go about creating a standard project, running it from the command line and importing it into your preferred IDE ready for development.

Coming up in the next chapter, we will look at making our very first LibGDX-based game! We will take a very well known old mobile game and recreate it in LibGDX. We will also introduce the game cycle concept along with rendering our own textures to the screen, move them, and access input detection.

2
Let's Get These Snakes Out of This Book!

In this chapter, we will start making our first game with the LibGDX framework. We will make a little journey back to one of the very first popular mobile games, Snake. We will start out by looking at LibGDX's update cycle and how textures are handled. Then, we will dive into the world of game making by creating our Snake game!

The following will be covered in this chapter:

- Why Snake?
- The game update cycle
- Introducing the snake
- Making the snake move
- Controlling the snake
- Introducing the collision detection mechanism
- Increasing the length of the snake once the apple is eaten

Why Snake?

Snake is one of the earliest mobile games that I can remember. I remember playing it many a time, chasing the apple while avoiding contact with the snake's own body. The beauty of the game was that it was a slightly different experience each time you played.

The premise is simple: navigate the snake around the board collecting apples — which increase the length of the snake when consumed — while avoiding collision with the snake itself.

Game update cycle

Before we jump straight into some coding action, let's first take a look at a couple of core classes that will make our lives easier. When you created your project with the setup tool, the core of the game, the MyGDXGame class, which is the default name of the class, extends a class called ApplicationAdapter. This in turn implements an interface called ApplicationListener. Now, you might think these are good enough for us to get going; however, there is a better class that we can extend and that is the Game class.

What is so special about this class? Essentially, it is ApplicationListener that delegates the game to a screen. Every bar method, such as onCreate(), is implemented. This will save us lots of time going forward.

The following code is the Game class from the LibGDX framework:

```java
public abstract class Game implements ApplicationListener {
   protected Screen screen;

   @Override
   public void dispose () {
      if (screen != null) screen.hide();
   }

   @Override
   public void pause () {
      if (screen != null) screen.pause();
   }

   @Override
   public void resume () {
      if (screen != null) screen.resume();
   }

   @Override
   public void render () {
      if (screen != null) screen.render(Gdx.graphics.getDeltaTime());
   }

   @Override
   public void resize (int width, int height) {
      if (screen != null) screen.resize(width, height);
   }

   public void setScreen (Screen screen) {
```

```
      if (this.screen != null) this.screen.hide();
      this.screen = screen;
      if (this.screen != null) {
        this.screen.show();
        this.screen.resize(Gdx.graphics.getWidth(), Gdx.graphics.
        getHeight());
      }
    }

  public Screen getScreen () {
    return screen;
  }
}
```

As we can see in the preceding code, the Game class is abstract, this will require us to provide our own implementation. Then, as mentioned earlier, it delegates life cycle calls to the Screen class.

The Screen class is used to define what a player is looking at, such as the main menu or the game screen. It has various methods that may be overridden. Let's take a look at the following code snippet:

```
public interface Screen {
  public void show ();
  public void render (float delta);
  public void resize (int width, int height);
  public void pause ();
  public void resume ();
  public void hide ();
  public void dispose ();
}
```

It has the same method signature as the ApplicationListener class. However, there is an additional method, show(), which is called when the screen becomes the current screen in the game.

We wouldn't want from implement all those methods every time we wanted to create a Screen class implementation. Luckily, LibGDX has an adapter class, ScreenAdapter, which is purely for convenience and contains zero logic. It implements the methods with empty bodies. I won't show the code structure here, I will leave it to you to look it up if you like.

Out of the life cycle methods that are mentioned here, we are only interested in a couple of these to start off with, show() and render().

The `render()` method is called on every cycle. By default, this is 60 times a second. This is configurable; however, we are happy with 60fps (frames per second) for now. In the default project, you will see that there is some interesting code already. What's happening here is that, with every frame, the screen is being cleared with the background color, which is red in this case, and rendering the LibGDX logo from scratch. This is achieved with the calls to `glClearColor()` and `glClear()`. Later, we will look at how we can clear with other colors.

Let's get our `Game` class up and running. Initially, it will not do much, but it will set us up to make our game.

First, let's generate a new project. This time, we will use some proper names as opposed to the defaults. To create the Snake game, we set the tool as follows:

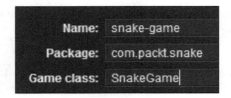

Once you have the project that is generated from the LibGDX setup application, import it into your IDE; if you are using Eclipse, refer to the previous chapter.

The `Game` class that is generated for you extends `ApplicationAdapter` by default.

```
public class SnakeGame extends ApplicationAdapter {
```

Let's change the extended class to `Game`:

```
public class SnakeGame extends Game {
```

Ensure that the imports are updated at the top of the class:

```
import com.badlogic.gdx.Game;
```

You will now notice that, essentially, nothing has changed. If you run the project again—via `DesktopLauncher`—it will still show the red screen with the LibGDX logo.

But why is this happening? We haven't set a `Screen` class for game object to use. The keen-eyed among you will have spotted that this is because we are still overriding the `render()` method. Thus, the delegation to the `Screen` class is not happening.

Before we remove the override, let's create our `Screen` class. Create a class called `GameScreen` and make it extend by the class `ScreenAdapter`:

```
public class GameScreen extends ScreenAdapter {
```

As all the interface methods are implemented in the `ScreenAdapter` class, you will notice that the IDE does not request that you implement anything.

Let's return to our `SnakeGame` class and remove the default project example code, so all we are left with is the `create()` method's override:

```
public class SnakeGame extends Game {
    @Override
    public void create() {
    }
}
```

In the `create()` method, we can set a new instance of our `GameScreen` method:

```
public class SnakeGame extends Game {
    @Override
    public void create() {
        setScreen(new GameScreen());
    }
}
```

If you run the project again, this time you will see that we just have a black screen; however, now the rendering is coming from the screen. Let's draw something on the screen!

Texture rendering

Now we have a blank screen, but let's make our screen do something! To start off with, let's put the default project code—the lovely LibGDX logo—onto the screen. You will notice that we don't have a `create()` method to put the object initialization in. We do, however, have a `show()` method. Let's put it in there. So now your `GameScreen` class should look something like this:

```
public class GameScreen extends ScreenAdapter {

    private SpriteBatch batch;
    private Texture img;

    @Override
```

```
    public void show() {

        batch = new SpriteBatch();
        img = new Texture("badlogic.jpg");
    }

    @Override
    public void render(float delta) {
        Gdx.gl.glClearColor(1, 0, 0, 1);
        Gdx.gl.glClear(GL20.GL_COLOR_BUFFER_BIT);
        batch.begin();
        batch.draw(img, 0, 0);
        batch.end();
    }
}
```

If you run the project again, you will see we are back to where we started. Before we go any further, I am going to provide a little explanation to what is going on, in the code, here.

The batch class

Next we need something that will draw our textures; this is where the batch classes come in. A Batch is used to draw 2D rectangles that reference a texture. Among the different Batch class implementations is SpriteBatch, which is the one we will use for our game.

The texture class

A texture is a bitmap image that gets drawn on the screen through mapping. The texture class wraps an OpenGL texture without having to worry too much about the internal workings of OpenGL—remember we are here to make games!

When using the texture class, we should ensure that our textures are managed; by this, we mean that if the OpenGL context is lost, for example, that loss can happen by the user switching to another application, then our managed textures will automatically get reloaded for us. Excellent!

The dispose() method

Everything we have talked about so far, somewhere in the inner workings of LibGDX, holds on to real resources, such as memory. To ensure that our games are well behaved and do not eat all available system memory, we have to remember to dispose of our SpriteBatch and textures when we are done using them. You will notice that they all have a `dispose()` method in them. When called, this will release all resources associated with that object. The `Screen` class has a `dispose()` method. We will look at that later on.

Introducing Sammy the snake

Before we start making the Snake game, we need to set up our textures for the snake and the game play area. So, let's remove the default code from our `GameScreen` class, leaving just our `SpriteBatch` batch's clear screen calls:

```
public class GameScreen extends ScreenAdapter {

    private SpriteBatch batch;

    @Override
    public void show() {
        batch = new SpriteBatch();
    }

    @Override
    public void render(float delta) {
        Gdx.gl.glClearColor(1, 0, 0, 1);
        Gdx.gl.glClear(GL20.GL_COLOR_BUFFER_BIT);
    }
}
```

Next, let's change the color that fills the screen from red to black. We can do this by updating the `glClearColor` method call to reference the r, g, b, a values of the black `Color` class:

```
Gdx.gl.glClearColor(Color.BLACK.r, Color.BLACK.g, Color.BLACK.b,
Color.BLACK.a);
```

If you run the project now, you will find that we are back to our black screen; however, this time, the screen is being cleared every render call. If you don't want to use black, check out the other default colors LibGDX provides, failing that you can define your own! You can do this by creating your own instance of `Color` with your own r, g, b, a values.

 We are very fortunate that there is now plenty of computing power available to do this. Many moons ago, game developers could only refresh sections of the screen that had changed to preserve CPU cycles.

Next we will add back calls in to our batch as we did earlier:

```
batch.begin();
//Our rendering code will live here!
batch.end();
```

Admittedly they won't do much right now, but our texture rendering code will sit in between them. Failing to call `begin()` before trying to call any other method for the `SpriteBatch` class will result in a `java.lang.IllegalStateException` exception being thrown.

Now, I think we are ready to start drawing our snake!

Giving the snake a face

We have two assets that we are going to use for drawing our snake, `snakehead.png` and `snakebody.png`. These assets will reside in a specific directory with in the project. As we are only using the desktop export of LibGDX at the moment, you will find an `assets` directory in the core project. However, when we start looking at the Android export, you will find the `assets` directory will move. The assets themselves are self-explanatory, one for the snakes head and one for the snakes body. Let's start with the head.

Back in our `GameScreen` class, add a texture object and call it `snakeHead`:

```
private Texture snakeHead;
```

Next, let's initialize the texture in the `show()` method:

```
snakeHead = new Texture(Gdx.files.internal("snakehead.png"));
```

Uh oh! Looks like something new cropped up here—`Gdx.files.internal`. LibGDX comes with some handy tools for handling files. Here we are just loading a file from within the project.

Now, let's render it in the `render()` method:

```
batch.draw(snakeHead,0,0);
```

Hopefully, when you run the project, you will get the following output:

The default resolution that the `DesktopLauncher` parameter has is 640 x 480 pixels. Currently, this is what we are rendering to. Later on, we will discuss using a viewport to allow us to handle multiple different resolutions.

Moving Sammy the snake

So, we have Sammy the snake on the screen, sitting there, looking snaky. However, it isn't much of a game. If it were, we could finish the book right here! What we need to do now is get that snake slithering across the screen!

First, let's sort out the playing area. Currently, the resolution is 640 x 480 pixels and the snake texture is 32 x 32. This means we have a grid of 20 x 15 — derived by dividing up the resolution by the texture *(640/32 = 20, 480/32 = 15)* — of the different positions the snake head could be in. The reason we are going to do it this way is because the original game moved with a periodic movement of one snake component at a time. We are going to do the same.

Let's define our timer. We are going to start off with an interval of one second between movements. So let's create a constant field:

```
private static final float MOVE_TIME = 1F;
```

Now, define a variable to keep track of the time:

```
private float timer = MOVE_TIME;
```

Finally, let's get it updated in every frame. This is in the `render()` method:

```
timer -= delta;
if (timer <= 0) {
    timer = MOVE_TIME;
}
```

Here we are deducting the time from the last frame. If the timer reaches zero or below, we reset it.

What we want to do next is move the snake head to the next block once the timer has reached zero or below. Since we only want to make the snake move right, we will be adding 32 px to the position of the snake.

Let's add an x and y component for the snake, and a constant for moving:

```
private static final int SNAKE_MOVEMENT = 32;
private int snakeX = 0, snakeY = 0;
```

Next, let's update the `render()` method:

```
@Override
public void render(float delta) {
    timer -= delta;
    if (timer <= 0) {
        timer = MOVE_TIME;
        snakeX += SNAKE_MOVEMENT;
    }
    Gdx.gl.glClearColor(Color.BLACK.r, Color.BLACK.g,
    Color.BLACK.b, Color.BLACK.a);
    Gdx.gl.glClear(GL20.GL_COLOR_BUFFER_BIT);
    batch.begin();
```

```
        batch.draw(snakeHead,snakeX,snakeY);
        batch.end();
    }
```

So now every time the timer reaches zero or below, the snake will move to the right by 32 px.

Run the default project and check it out!

So what did you see? Hopefully, it was the snake head scrolling across the screen in intervals of 1 second. Then it probably disappeared off to the right? Yes, we should have been expecting that. We told the snake head to move to the right indefinitely. What we should do, staying true to the original, is have the snake reappear on the left-hand side.

Let's create a method to check for the position of the snake:

```
private void checkForOutOfBounds() {
    if (snakeX >= Gdx.graphics.getWidth()) {
        snakeX = 0;
    }
}
```

Now we should have this method called after we move the snake. What we are doing here is checking whether the position of the snake head is outside the screen. We do this by querying the screen's width and checking whether the snake's x position is greater than or equal to it. We then reset it to zero.

Running the project now, you will see that the snake head will return back to the start of the screen.

This is all well and good, but again, it isn't much of a game just having the snake move to the right. What we need to do is give the snake a direction:

```
private static final int RIGHT = 0;
private static final int LEFT = 1;
private static final int UP = 2;
private static final int DOWN = 3;
private int snakeDirection = RIGHT;
```

By adding some constants and a variable, we can keep track of the snake's direction. Now that we have a direction, we need to be more precise on how we mean to move the snake. Let's replace the current code for moving with the following method:

```
private void moveSnake() {
    switch (snakeDirection) {
        case RIGHT: {
```

```
                 snakeX += SNAKE_MOVEMENT;
                 return;
            }
            case LEFT: {
                 snakeX -= SNAKE_MOVEMENT;
                 return;
            }
            case UP: {
                 snakeY += SNAKE_MOVEMENT;
                 return;
            }
            case DOWN: {
                 snakeY -= SNAKE_MOVEMENT;
                 return;
            }
        }
    }
```

Now, depending the direction set, the snake will move; give it a go and set the snake to move in a different direction.

Ah, I bet you've seen the problem with this already. We only check whether the snake is on the screen when moving right, and that means we need to update our bounds to check method to cover all cases:

```
private void checkForOutOfBounds() {
    if (snakeX >= Gdx.graphics.getWidth()) {
        snakeX = 0;
    }
    if (snakeX < 0) {
        snakeX = Gdx.graphics.getWidth() - SNAKE_MOVEMENT;
    }
    if (snakeY >= Gdx.graphics.getHeight()) {
        snakeY = 0;
    }
    if (snakeY < 0) {
        snakeY = Gdx.graphics.getHeight() - SNAKE_MOVEMENT;
    }
}
```

That should be better!

Just before we move on to controlling the snake, let's do a little code refactor to stop things from getting a bit too messy in our render() method. You will see in the samples that this has already been done!

Controlling Sammy with event polling

Now we are going to look at how to control our snake. Normally, there are a couple of approaches to handle user input. One is event polling, where we can query the state of the input and then update our game accordingly. Generally, this polling will occur during the main game loop, just before the rendering. The other method is to listen to events; we register a listener that will receive events from the LibGDX framework when the player interacts with the game, that is, presses a key. For now, we will just work with polling.

As we are working in desktop mode, we will take advantage of the arrow keys on the keyboard. Because LibGDX is so awesome, there is a really convenient way to poll for user input, `Gdx.input`. There is a vast array of methods that we can call here to determine what the player has pressed. For this example, we will be focus on the `Gdx.input.isKeyPressed()` method. Here we can specify the key to query by passing in a key code. The codes are available as constants that live inside the `Keys` static class; please check the official documentation at `http://libgdx.badlogicgames.com/nightlies/docs/api/com/badlogic/gdx/Input.Keys.html` to access the whole list.

So how do we use it?

Well, let's create a method called `queryInput()` in it. We will check whether the arrow keys have been pressed and update the snake direction accordingly:

```
private void queryInput() {
    boolean lPressed = Gdx.input.isKeyPressed(Input.Keys.LEFT);
    boolean rPressed = Gdx.input.isKeyPressed(Input.Keys.RIGHT);
    boolean uPressed = Gdx.input.isKeyPressed(Input.Keys.UP);
    boolean dPressed = Gdx.input.isKeyPressed(Input.Keys.DOWN);

    if (lPressed) snakeDirection = LEFT;
    if (rPressed) snakeDirection = RIGHT;
    if (uPressed) snakeDirection = UP;
    if (dPressed) snakeDirection = DOWN;
}
```

So firstly, we query the four keys we are interested in, and then we set the direction.

Now, add this method to the top of the `render()` method.

Run the project and you will find that you can control the snake with the arrow keys.

Adding the apple

Next up, we need to get our snake eating something. Let's get our apple implemented.

We will need to get our apple to do the following things:

- Randomly being placed on the screen, not on the snake!
- Only place one if there isn't an apple on the screen already
- Disappear when it collides with the snake's head

Right! Let's add the texture:

```
private Texture apple;
```

Then, let's amend our `show()` method and add the code to instantiate the apple texture:

```
apple = new Texture(Gdx.files.internal("apple.png"));
```

Let's add a flag to determine if the apple is available:

```
private boolean appleAvailable = false;
private int appleX, appleY;
```

This will control whether or not we want to place one. In the Snake game, the next apple appears after the current apple is eaten; therefore, we don't need any fancy timing mechanism to deal with it. Hence, the apple is not available at the start as we need to place one first. We also specify the variables that will contain the location of the apple.

Finally, add the drawing code to the `render()` method:

```
if (appleAvailable) {
    batch.draw(apple, appleX, appleY);
}
```

Here, we tell the game to only render the apple if it has been placed.

Now we need to randomly place the apple on the screen:

```
private void checkAndPlaceApple() {
    if (!appleAvailable) {
        do {
            appleX = MathUtils.random(Gdx.graphics.getWidth()
            / SNAKE_MOVEMENT - 1) * SNAKE_MOVEMENT;
            appleY = MathUtils.random(Gdx.graphics.getHeight()
            / SNAKE_MOVEMENT - 1) * SNAKE_MOVEMENT;
```

```
        appleAvailable = true;
    } while (appleX == snakeX && appleY == snakeY);
    }
}
```

The previous code listing shows the required rule for placing the apple on the screen. First, we check whether we need to place an apple, then we randomly pick a location on the screen, which is a multiple of 32, and we repick it if the picked location contains the snake. As we are working in a 0-indexed environment we need to subtract one (1-20 becomes 0-19 and 1-15 becomes 0-14). Add this method to the render() method after we move the snake:

```
@Override
public void render(float delta) {
    queryInput();
    timer -= delta;
    if (timer <= 0) {
        timer = MOVE_TIME;
        moveSnake();
        checkForOutOfBounds();
    }
    checkAndPlaceApple();
    clearScreen();
    draw();
}
```

You may have noticed two new methods creep in there, clearScreen() and draw(). These are the result of a very quick refactor to neaten up our render method. The clearScreen() method is as follows:

```
private void clearScreen() {
    Gdx.gl.glClearColor(Color.BLACK.r, Color.BLACK.g,
    Color.BLACK.b, Color.BLACK.a);
    Gdx.gl.glClear(GL20.GL_COLOR_BUFFER_BIT);
}
```

The draw() method is as follows:

```
private void draw() {
    batch.begin();
    batch.draw(snakeHead, snakeX, snakeY);
    if (appleAvailable) {
        batch.draw(apple, appleX, appleY);
    }
    batch.end();
}
```

Now run the project. Hopefully you will see something similar to the following screenshot. The apple will be randomly placed on the screen every time you launch the project.

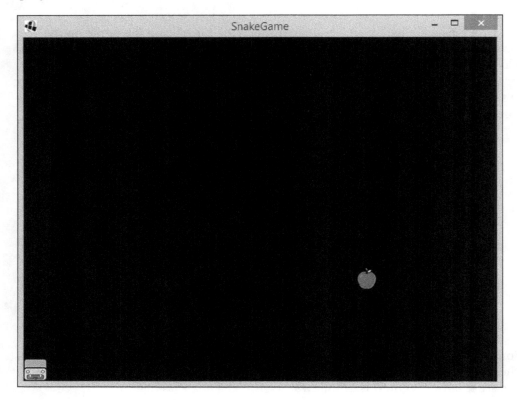

You may have noticed, however, that if you take control of the snake and head over to the apple, the snake will just glide over the top and the apple will remain. Not very game-like and not what we would want to happen.

Let's fix this!

We can do this quite simply by checking whether the apple and the snake head coordinates match:

```
private void checkAppleCollision() {
    if (appleAvailable && appleX == snakeX && appleY == snakeY) {
        appleAvailable = false;
    }
}
```

If they do collide, we set the `appleAvailable` flag to `false`. This will trigger a respawn of the apple.

Add the `checkAppleCollision()` method to the `render()` method above `checkAndPlaceApple()`.

Run the project, and you will now find that the apple respawns every time the snakes head collides with it.

On to the final part of this chapter. We need to make the snake grow in length every time it eats an apple.

Increasing the length of the snake

We have the snake eating the apple; however, there aren't any consequences to this. As a part of the game, we need to make the snake increase the length of his body for each apple he eats. Our requirements for this are as follows:

- Add a body part to the snake when it eats an apple
- As the snake moves, the body parts should follow
- There will be multiple body parts

First, let's create a class that will contain the length of the snake's body. This can take the form of an inner class for now:

```
private class BodyPart {

    private int x, y;
    private Texture texture;

    public BodyPart(Texture texture) {
        this.texture = texture;
    }

    public void updateBodyPosition(int x, int y) {
        this.x = x;
        this.y = y;
    }

    public void draw(Batch batch) {
        if (!(x == snakeX && y == snakeY)) batch.draw(texture,
        x, y);
    }
}
```

As you can see, it contains the x and y components along with the texture to be drawn. It also has a `draw()` method which will only draw the texture if the body part is not in the same location as the snake's head. This is important for when you collect the apple; you wouldn't want the body part showing over the head before the snake moves.

Next, let's create the texture:

```
private Texture snakeBody;
```

Again in our `show()` method, let's add code to instantiate the object:

```
snakeBody = new Texture(Gdx.files.internal("snakeBody.png"));
```

Let's create an array of body parts:

```
private Array<BodyPart> bodyParts = new Array<BodyPart>();
```

Here, we are using LibGDX's built-in `Array<T>` class. It has some useful methods for accessing the the first and last element of the array that we will need shortly.

Now, when that part is set up, we can add a body part when a collision between the snakes head and apple occurs:

```
private void checkAppleCollision() {
    if (appleAvailable && appleX == snakeX && appleY == snakeY) {
        BodyPart bodyPart = new BodyPart(snakeBody);
        bodyPart.updateBodyPosition(snakeX, snakeY);
        bodyParts.insert(0,bodyPart);
        appleAvailable = false;
    }
}
```

When a collision is detected, we create a new body part, set its position, and insert it at the front of the array. We are reusing the texture for the body parts, so we can reduce our memory footprint by not loading it multiple times. We can do this as the drawing of the texture doesn't require it to be a different instance of the texture every time we draw it in the same render cycle.

Next, we need to update the body parts every time the snake moves; if we don't do this, they will remain in their place for all eternity. Let's add the following code to our game:

```
private int snakeXBeforeUpdate = 0, snakeYBeforeUpdate = 0;
private void moveSnake() {
    snakeXBeforeUpdate = snakeX;
    snakeYBeforeUpdate = snakeY;
```

```
        // Rest of method omitted
    }
    private void updateBodyPartsPosition() {
        if (bodyParts.size > 0) {
            BodyPart bodyPart = bodyParts.removeIndex(0);
            bodyPart.updateBodyPosition(snakeXBeforeUpdate,
            snakeYBeforeUpdate);
            bodyParts.add(bodyPart);
        }
    }
```

Right, first we need to keep track of the previous position of the snake—the reason for this will be clear in a minute. Then we have the `updateBodyPartsPosition()` method, where we take the front element of the array, which would be the body part that is the tail part of the snake, and we remove it from the array. We then update the position and add it to the back of the array, which is the front of the snake. This means we are only updating the one body part as the others won't need to move unless they are the tail of the snake.

Add a call to this method after we check whether the snake is out of bounds:

```
        // render method
    moveSnake();
    checkForOutOfBounds();
    updateBodyPartsPosition();
```

Before we run the project and see what we have created, we need to update our `draw()` method to draw out the body of the snake:

```
    private void draw() {
      batch.begin();
      batch.draw(snakeHead, snakeX, snakeY);
      for (BodyPart bodyPart : bodyParts) {
        bodyPart.draw(batch);
      }
      if (appleAvailable) {
        batch.draw(apple, appleX, appleY);
      }
      batch.end();
    }
```

With that in place, if you run the project now, you will see that the snake grows every time it eats an apple.

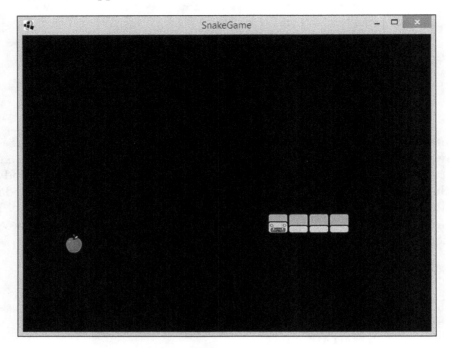

Summary

In this chapter, we looked at setting up our game to use the screen-based system, we then implemented our own game using the Game class. We looked at the render cycle and the loaded textures and handled input. We have the makings of a very good game!

Coming up, we will take this game further and make it complete. We will do this by adding the collision of the snake with itself, creating a gameover scenario, and introducing a scoring system.

3
Making That Snake Slick

In this chapter, we will take our Snake project further towards being a complete game. This will include more on collisions, restarting the game, and maintaining a high score. You will also learn how to use LibGDX to help in making it easier to debug your game along with how to handle multiple screen sizes.

The following will be covered in this chapter:

- Introducing the `ShapeRenderer` class
- More on collisions
- Game state
- High score
- Handling different screen sizes

Introducing the ShapeRenderer class

You are probably wondering why we are not diving straight into making more improvements to the game. Well, it is because I would like to show you something that will make your life easier when you start making more games, especially if you don't have any art ready for the game you are making and you want to see things come to life sooner. As an eager game developer myself, I know what that is like; you have an idea and you want to bring it to life faster than your artist can design, draw, and deliver. Alternatively, in the case of our Snake game, we can draw the grid that our snake moves in.

So, I introduce you to the `ShapeRenderer` class; its job is simple. According to `http://libgdx.badlogicgames.com/nightlies/docs/api/com/badlogic/gdx/graphics/glutils/ShapeRenderer.html`, the `ShapeRenderer` class does the following:

"Renders points, lines, shape outlines and filled shapes."

This means we will have the ability to draw boxes on the screen. Let's put this into our Snake game so you can see it in action.

Adding the ShapeRenderer class

The first thing to do is to add the `ShapeRenderer` class to our `GameScreen` class. The following code shows how to add and create a `ShapeRenderer` object:

```
private ShapeRenderer shapeRenderer;

@Override
public void show() {
  shapeRenderer = new ShapeRenderer();
  // Other code omitted for now
}
```

We now have a `ShapeRenderer` object ready to go!

Drawing with the ShapeRenderer class

Well, it is great that we have it, but how do we use it? The `ShapeRenderer` class has quite a few drawing methods available, giving it the ability to draw arcs, circles, cones, rectangles, lines, and more. However, right now we are only interested in using it for drawing rectangles.

When using the `ShaperRenderer` class, much like the `SpriteBatch` class, we need to call the drawing methods in a particular order, which is as follows:

1. Begin a new batch.
2. Draw our shapes.
3. Finish our batch and ensure they get rendered.

First, let's create a method to draw our grid; again, this is all happening in our `GameScreen` class:

```
private void drawGrid() {
}
```

Let's now add our begin and end calls:

```
private void drawGrid() {
    shapeRenderer.begin(ShapeRenderer.ShapeType.Line);
    shapeRenderer.end();
}
```

You may have noticed that the begin method call takes a parameter of type `ShapeRenderer.ShapeType`. This is because we need to tell the `ShapeRenderer` object what type of shape we are going to render. We only want to draw the outline of our shapes, or rectangles in our case, so we can use the `Line` type. There are others as well; feel free to experiment to see what happens if you choose one of the others!

Next, we need to draw our grid; to do this, we need to know what our grid is. Our grid comprises of squares that are 32x32 pixels in size, and we will want to render one of these squares ever 32 pixels both horizontally and vertically. We can achieve this by two simple loops. The following code shows this implementation:

```
private void drawGrid() {
    shapeRenderer.begin(ShapeRenderer.ShapeType.Line);
    for (int x = 0; x < Gdx.graphics.getWidth(); x += GRID_CELL) {
        for (int y = 0; y < Gdx.graphics.getHeight(); y += GRID_CELL) {
            shapeRenderer.rect(x,y, GRID_CELL, GRID_CELL);
        }
    }
    shapeRenderer.end();
}
```

The call itself to `ShapeRenderer` is fairly self-explanatory:

```
shapeRenderer.rect(x,y, GRID_CELL, GRID_CELL);
```

It takes four parameters, that is, the x and y coordinates and the width and height. Since we want a square, our width and height values will be the same.

We have also introduced a constant field to define the size of our cell:

```
private static final int GRID_CELL = 32;
```

Finally, we just need to update our `render()` method so that it calls our `drawGrid()` method:

```
public void render(float delta) {
        // Other code omitted for now
    drawGrid();
    draw();
}
```

Now, when you run your project, you will see the following:

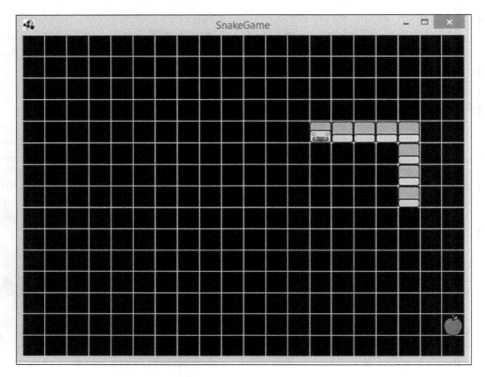

We now have a working grid!

Final thoughts on the ShapeRenderer class

As I mentioned earlier in this chapter, the `ShaperRenderer` class is very useful when you want to make a game and you do not have your art assets ready; you want to quickly prototype the game; or, in our case, you want to make things a bit clearer in the game you're currently creating.

Finally, another useful aspect is being able to set the color of the shapes that are drawn. The method call is `setColor()` and I use it do draw different game objects in different colors, so I can tell them apart!

More on collisions

You might have found while playing our little game that you can make the snake turn back on itself or it even goes through itself. Anyone who remembers the original will know that this results in an immediate game over!

What we are going to look at now can essentially be split into two parts. First, we will fix the snake's ability to slither back on itself, as seen in the following screenshot:

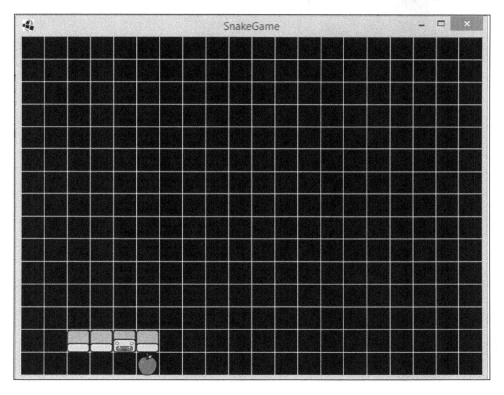

Second, we will look at stopping the game when the snake collides with another part of its body, as seen in the following screenshot:

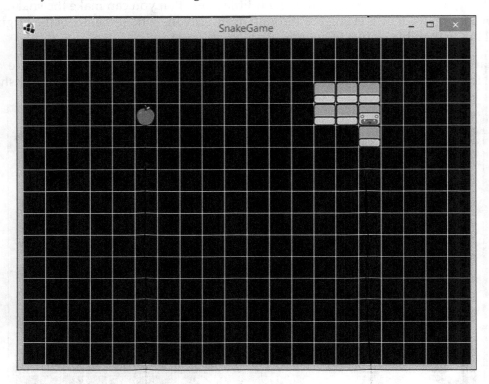

Stopping the doubleback

With our snake slithering around, if you change the direction of the snake and you tell it to go back the way it is traveling, it will slide right through itself. This isn't how the game should be!

Essentially, what we want to do is, if the player tells the snake to change its direction and move in the exact opposite direction, ignore that input command.

First, we will create a method to do this precise check:

```
private void updateIfNotOppositeDirection(int newSnakeDirection, int
oppositeDirection) {
    if (snakeDirection != oppositeDirection) snakeDirection =
newSnakeDirection;
}
```

What we will pass into this method is the new direction that we would like to send the snake in, but then also the opposite direction (left and right or up and down) so we make the check and only update the direction if it isn't the opposite.

Next, we create a method that will call `updateIfNotOppositeDirection()` with all the possible combinations. We are lucky there are only four!

The following method shows how we will do this:

```
private void updateDirection(int newSnakeDirection) {
    if (!directionSet && snakeDirection != newSnakeDirection) {
        directionSet = true;
        switch (newSnakeDirection) {
          case LEFT: {
              updateIfNotOppositeDirection(newSnakeDirection, RIGHT);
          }
          break;
          case RIGHT: {
              updateIfNotOppositeDirection(newSnakeDirection, LEFT);
          }
          break;
          case UP: {
              updateIfNotOppositeDirection(newSnakeDirection, DOWN);
          }
          break;
          case DOWN: {
              updateIfNotOppositeDirection(newSnakeDirection, UP);
          }
          break;
        }
    }
}
```

Now, to take a little side step, you may have noticed that I have introduced a new member to the GameScreen class here: directionSet — a Boolean flag. This is needed because of how we poll for input compared to the snake update. The snake currently has its movement updated periodically, currently every half a second, yet we poll for input at a rate of up to 1/60th of a second. This means our snake's direction can change up to 30 times before it moves! This would allow a player to negate what we are trying to stop — the snake turning back on itself.

So what we do is, once we detect a new input after we move the snake, we take that input. However, we take it if the newSnakeDirection value is not equal to that of the current snakeDirection value.

We reset the `directionSet` flag after we move the snake.

Finally, we update our `quertInput()` method to call our new `updateDirection()` method:

```
private void queryInput() {
    boolean lPressed = Gdx.input.isKeyPressed(Input.Keys.LEFT);
    boolean rPressed = Gdx.input.isKeyPressed(Input.Keys.RIGHT);
    boolean uPressed = Gdx.input.isKeyPressed(Input.Keys.UP);
    boolean dPressed = Gdx.input.isKeyPressed(Input.Keys.DOWN);

    if (lPressed) updateDirection(LEFT);
    if (rPressed) updateDirection(RIGHT);
    if (uPressed) updateDirection(UP);
    if (dPressed) updateDirection(DOWN);
}
```

If you now launch the game, you will see that the snake can now no longer slither back onto itself!

However, did you notice the deliberate mistake I've included?

If you try to change to the opposite direction while the snake is only a head, it won't let you! Try it, go ahead!

To fix this, we need to update our `updateIfNotOppositeDirection()` method to also check on the size of the snake, as follows:

```
private void updateIfNotOppositeDirection(int newSnakeDirection, int oppositeDirection) {
    if (snakeDirection != oppositeDirection || bodyParts.size == 0)
snakeDirection = newSnakeDirection;
}
```

Now try it. You will find that it is all fixed!

Colliding with the body

On to the second part of this topic. We will now look into stopping the game when the snake collides with itself. To achieve this, we will need to do a few things:

- Introduce a collision flag
- Check the snake's head position compared to its body parts
- Update the collision flag when there is a collision
- Stop the movement of the snake if the flag returns `true`

First, let's introduce the flag:

```
private boolean hasHit = false;
```

Add this flag to the GameScreen class. We will update it later!

Next, we need to check for the collision. This is fairly straightforward, as we know the location of our snake's body parts and head. Let's create a method called checkSnakeBodyCollision() in our GameScreen class:

```
private void checkSnakeBodyCollision() {
    for (BodyPart bodyPart : bodyParts) {
        if (bodyPart.x == snakeX && bodyPart.y == snakeY) hasHit = true;
    }
}
```

The preceding code checks whether the *x* and *y* coordinates of our snake's head match its body parts. If true, let's set our flag. Simple!

We now add this method call to our updateSnake() method block:

```
private void updateSnake(float delta) {
    timer -= delta;
    if (timer <= 0) {
        timer = MOVE_TIME;
    moveSnake();
    checkForOutOfBounds();
    updateBodyPartsPosition();
    checkSnakeBodyCollision();
    directionSet = false;
    }
}
```

Finally, to complete this, we add a check on our flag before we go on to update our snake.

```
private void updateSnake(float delta) {
    if (!hasHit) {
      //Update snake code omitted
    }
}
```

Now if you launch the game, you will see that it will appear to stop when you make the snake collide with its body.

We almost have a complete game on our hands!

The state of the game

We now have our Snake game at the point where it is almost a complete game; we just need to add a few more things to achieve this. Currently, our game stops when the snake collides with itself. What we need to add is a way to restart the game if this happens, so the player can have another go!

To do this, we will do the following:

- Adding a game state
- Displaying game-over text
- Restarting the game

Adding a state

When you think about it, a game can have many states. Seriously, pick one of your favorite games and consider the states the game could be in. Let's list some out:

- Start
- Playing
- Paused
- Game over
- Restart

It could be argued that start and restart are the same thing, but that really depends on the game and what you, as the game developer, would like to achieve. For our little Snake game, we are only going to focus on two states for now: playing and game over.

Let's first start off by creating an enumeration of our states, and let's create a member of GameScreen to use it:

```
private enum STATE {
    PLAYING, GAME_OVER
}

private STATE state = STATE.PLAYING;
```

By default, our game will start in the playing state, no different than how it is now!

Next, let's update our `render()` method to take this new state into consideration:

```
public void render(float delta) {
    switch(state) {
        case PLAYING: {
            queryInput();
            updateSnake(delta);
            checkAppleCollision();
            checkAndPlaceApple();
        }
        break;
        case GAME_OVER: {

        }
        break;
    }
    clearScreen();
    drawGrid();
    draw();
}
```

What we have achieved here is, essentially, only updating the game state while in playing mode. What this means is that we can now do away with that code-invasive `hasHit` flag, as we can now change the state of the game to GAME_OVER instead!

Let's update our `checkSnakeBodyCollision()` method to reflect this:

```
private void checkSnakeBodyCollision() {
    for (BodyPart bodyPart : bodyParts) {
        if (bodyPart.x == snakeX && bodyPart.y == snakeY) state =
STATE.GAME_OVER;
    }
}
```

Now run the game. It should run exactly as it did earlier! The exception is that we now enter the GAME_OVER state on collision.

Player feedback

Now that we have the game set up to handle different states, let's provide the player with some feedback to the effect that they lost (aww) our little Snake game. Once you get comfortable with making games, particularly with the LibGDX framework, you can really make some amazing things happen in the game-over scenario. However, for our game, we will just display some text.

How are we going to achieve this? Luckily, for us, LibGDX has bitmap font support, so we can go ahead and start drawing text on the screen. By default, LibGDX comes with Arial font at size 15, which will do for now.

To use this bitmap font, we need to define and then create an instance in our `GameScreen` class, once again in the `show()` method; we update it as follows:

```
private BitmapFont bitmapFont;

public void show() {
    bitmapFont = new BitmapFont();
    // other code omitted
}
```

Next, we will make it draw some text to the screen. Let's update our `draw()` method with a call to the draw method of our font:

```
private void draw() {
    batch.begin();
    //Other render code omitted
    bitmapFont.draw(batch, "This Snake Game is AWESOME!", 0, 0);
    batch.end();
}
```

The `bitmapFont.draw()` method signature shows that it requires a `batch` object, the text, and the location to start at. Let's place it in the bottom-left corner for now!

Let's run our game and see our text on the screen!

Oh, it didn't render! Well, technically it would have, if it had been on screen. However, what I didn't point out is that it renders the text from the top-left corner rather than the bottom-left corner, as with our game textures.

The question is, How do we know where to draw it then, as different fonts will have different widths and heights? Well, we have to define an instance of a class called `GlyphLayout`. This class allows us to obtain the size of the string we wish to display. Perfect!

Let's update our code to utilize this then. First let's define the `GlyphLayout` class:

```
private GlyphLayout layout = new GlyphLayout();
```

Next, we then set the text which we have to use.

```
String text = "This Snake Game is AWESOME!";
layout.setText(text);
bitmapFont.draw(batch, text, 0, layout.height);
```

What is happening here is that we are using the height of our font as the *y* coordinate to start the render from. Run the game and see for yourself. The text will now appear where we expected it to, and hopefully will look like the following screenshot:

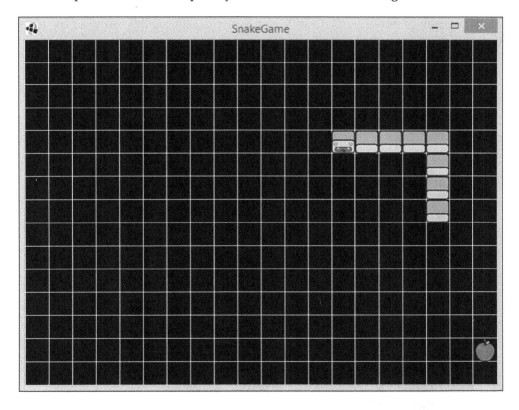

However, as awesome as this is, this isn't what we are looking to achieve. What we are aiming to do is to have the text displayed when the game is over.

First, let's add a constant value with our game-over message, again in the
`GameScreen` class:

```
private static final String GAME_OVER_TEXT = "Game Over!";
```

Finally, in our `draw()` method, we can update this to draw our text when in the
`GAME_OVER` state:

```
if (state == STATE.GAME_OVER) {
  layout.setText(bitmapFont, GAME_OVER_TEXT);
  bitmapFont.draw(batch, GAME_OVER_TEXT, (viewport.getWorldWidth() -
layout.width) / 2, (viewport.getWorldHeight() - layout.height) / 2);
}
```

The position at which we are setting the render of the font is the center of the screen,
offset by the size of the text.

Let's run the game and get to a `GAME_OVER` state to see our text!

But before we do that, let's turn off the `drawGrid()` call so it doesn't get in the way!
We can simply just comment it for now.

Hopefully, your game will look as shown in the following screenshot:

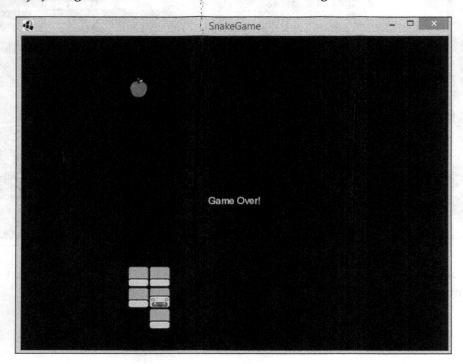

Restart your engines!

So, the player now knows that they have lost the game. However, what if they want to play again? More complex games will have different flows through which they might want to take the player during a restart scenario of the game. However, for us, we just want to have the game set itself back up and let the player go again!

First, let's define how to restart the game. Let's use the space bar to restart the game. Now, create a method called `checkForRestart()` and another called `doRestart()` in our `GameScreen` class. Inside it, we will query the input for the space bar:

```
private void checkForRestart() {
    if (Gdx.input.isKeyPressed(Input.Keys.SPACE)) doRestart();
}

private void doRestart() {
    state = STATE.PLAYING;
    bodyParts.clear();
    snakeDirection = RIGHT;
    directionSet = false;
    timer = MOVE_TIME;
    snakeX = 0;
    snakeY = 0;
    snakeXBeforeUpdate = 0;
    snakeYBeforeUpdate = 0;
    appleAvailable = false;
}
```

As you can see in our `doRestart()` method, we are resetting the game logic. This will put everything back to how it was when the game launched.

Finally, add a call to the `checkForRestart()` method in the `GAME_OVER` case in our `render()` call:

```
case GAME_OVER: {
    checkForRestart();
}
```

Let's run the game again. Now when we enter the `GAME_OVER` state, if we press the spacebar, the game will reset! Perfect!

As a final touch, we should update our `GAME_OVER_TEXT` constant to let the player know how to restart, as follows:

```
private static final String GAME_OVER_TEXT = "Game Over... Tap space
to restart!";
```

Now your game over should look like this:

High scores

One of the final pieces is still missing from our Snake game; we don't have, or keep track of, any scoring! How is the player supposed to know how well they did when the game finishes?

The first step to solve this is to add a member to the GameScreen class called score, which we will add to the following:

```
private int score = 0;
```

But how much should we add? It is completely up to you, the game designer, how many points you want to give to the player. For the sake of simplicity, let's just say 20 points per apple collected. Feel free to change this later to whatever you like. Let's create a constant member:

```
private static final int POINTS_PER_APPLE = 20;
```

Next, let's create a method that can be called every time a player makes the snake collide with the apple:

```
private void addToScore() {
    score += POINTS_PER_APPLE;
}
```

Now, we need to find a logical place to call this method. What we can do is place this method call inside the checkAppleCollision() method call, as follows:

```
private void checkAppleCollision() {
    if (appleAvailable && appleX == snakeX && appleY == snakeY) {
        BodyPart bodyPart = new BodyPart(snakeBody);
        bodyPart.updateBodyPosition(snakeX, snakeY);
        bodyParts.insert(0, bodyPart);
        addToScore();
        appleAvailable = false;
    }
}
```

Let's run the game and see what happens.

You probably have guessed, or noticed, right away that, although the code might be keeping track of the score, we have no way of feeding that back to the user.

What we can do to fix this is have the score displayed to the user as the game is being played—like a real game!

To do this, we need to update the draw() method call to draw our score out, so let's create the following method to do this:

```
private void drawScore() {
    if (state == STATE.PLAYING) {
        String scoreAsString = Integer.toString(score);
        BitmapFont.TextBounds scoreBounds = bitmapFont.
        getBounds(scoreAsString);
        bitmapFont.draw(batch, scoreAsString, (Gdx.graphics.getWidth()
        - scoreBounds.width) / 2, (4 * Gdx.graphics.getHeight() / 5) -
        scoreBounds.height / 2);
    }
}
```

What we are saying here is: if the game state is playing, convert the integer score to a string object. Then, we create a TextBounds instance so we know the size of our string in terms of the font. Finally, we make the call to draw it to the screen, in the middle and slightly higher up the screen.

Next, add the method call to our original `draw()` method:

```
private void draw() {
    batch.begin();
    // Other render code ommited for brevity
    drawScore();
    batch.end();
}
```

If we now run the game, we should see the score on the screen, and it will go up every time we make the snake eat the apple. Excellent!

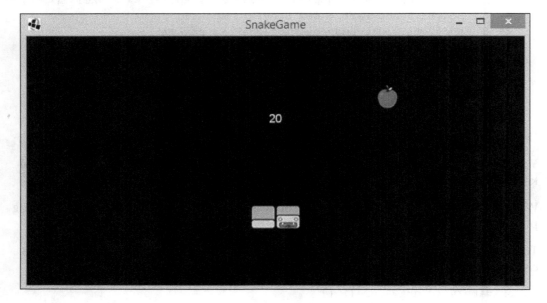

I hope you had a good play and reached a high score; however, you probably have noticed a bug in the game! Yes, that's right; we don't reset the score when we restart the game. This mean a player can grow their score indefinitely! Let's update our `doRestart()` method to reset the score:

```
private void doRestart() {
    // Other code ommited for brevity
    score = 0;
}
```

Now it will reset and the player will start from zero every time!

Handling different screen sizes

On to the final topic of this chapter. One important aspect of game development that needs to be addressed, especially in the world of mobile gaming, is the varying screen sizes that a game can be played on.

Currently, our Snake game is just running against whatever native screen size we have configured in our `DesktopLauncher` class. If you look at this you will see that in fact we haven't configured any; we have just used the default LibGDX desktop configuration of 640 x 480 pixels.

You might now be wondering why this actually matters. Let's take our Snake game as an example. We currently create a grid of 32 x 32 pixels in which our snake moves around. If the screen size is suddenly doubled, our grid will double in size too. This means it would take the snake twice as long to traverse the screen than it took earlier. However, also consider what would would happen if the screen size was half that size; in that case, the grid would also be half the size.

Maybe this is what you might want in your game, or maybe it isn't. From my experience, I can tell you it probably isn't what you want.

If you want to play about with the screen size, feel free. You can change the values on the `LwjglApplicationConfiguration` class as follows:

```
public static void main (String[] arg) {
    LwjglApplicationConfiguration config = new
    LwjglApplicationConfiguration();
    config.width = 640;
    config.height = 480;
    new LwjglApplication(new SnakeGame(), config);
}
```

I suggest that you try different values and see how it changes the game. If you like, enable the code to draw the grid on the screen. You should find that, at 640 x 480, we have 20 cells going across; if you double the screen size, it is now 40! You can try out different aspect ratios as well. You will even find that, if you use values that are not a multiple of our cell size, 32, the game won't work properly!

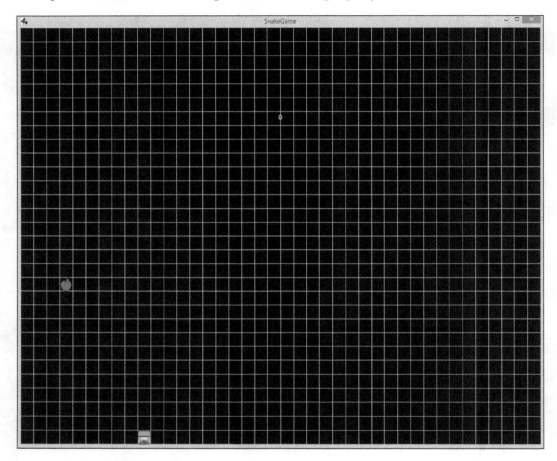

In the preceding screenshot, you can see that the game world in which our snake lives in is now twice the size. I set our screen size to be 1280x960 pixels.

Introducing the Viewport

You may want to have a stable playing environment regardless of screen size. Well, let's talk about how we can achieve this. We can do this by creating a Viewport instance and a camera instance.

First, what is a viewport?

In LibGDX terms, it is a way to manage a camera, mapping screen coordinates to the games world's coordinates. LibGDX comes with the following Viewport implementations, but you can also create your own:

- StretchViewport
- FitViewport
- FillViewport
- ScreenViewport
- ExtendedViewport
- CustomViewport

 I am not going to discuss each at length here; you can visit the LibGDX wiki at `https://github.com/libgdx/libgdx/wiki/Viewports` to see them in action.

I suppose the next logical question you are now asking is, "What's a camera?"

Again, in LibGDX, a camera gives us the ability to change the player's view on the world. We can create a camera and use it to zoom in and out, rotate, and project points to/from the screen to the world space.

LibGDX has two camera implementations:

- Orthographic
- Perspective

We are going to focus solely on the first one, as the latter is used for 3D.

 For more information on the orthographic camera, you can check out the LibGDX wiki at `https://github.com/libgdx/libgdx/wiki/Orthographic-camera`.

Using the Viewport

Now that we know of the existence of viewports, let's get one into our Snake game.

First, we need to declare our world size. This is what the camera and Viewport will work to when displaying the game world to the player. So, let's add the following to our GameScreen class:

```
private static final float WORLD_WIDTH = 640;
private static final float WORLD_HEIGHT = 480;
```

Now, what I am going to say might sound a touch confusing. We need to stop thinking in pixels. I know, I know, what did we just define? A world of 640 x 480. But these dimensions aren't pixels now; the screen size is pixels and these could be anything. These are just units: the player's view on the world is going to be 640 units wide and 480 units high.

Next, let's define our viewport and camera:

```
private Viewport viewport;
private Camera camera;

public void show() {
   camera = new OrthographicCamera(Gdx.graphics.getWidth(),
   Gdx.graphics.getHeight());
   camera.position.set(WORLD_WIDTH / 2, WORLD_HEIGHT / 2, 0);
   camera.update();
   viewport = new FitViewport(WORLD_WIDTH, WORLD_HEIGHT, camera);
   //Other code ommited for brevity
}
```

So, what we have done here is initialize a camera and point it to the center of our game world. We then tell it to call update(), which recalculates the camera's projection and view. This needs to be done any time we interact with the camera ourselves.

Finally, we instantiate a FitViewport viewport class. Why FitViewport? Well, this will maintain the aspect ratio of the game world irrespective of the screen size. The only downside is you may get a black bar border—similar to what you get when you watch old 4:3 TV shows on your 16:9 TV.

Next, we need to do a little-find-and replace. Previously, we used the following lines of code to access the screen size:

```
Gdx.graphics.getWidth()
Gdx.graphics.getHeight()
```

However, these return the actual screen size, something we no longer work in. So we need to replace these references with the following:

```
viewport.getWorldWidth()
viewport.getWorldHeight()
```

You will notice some errors pop up. These will be related to the phase we have gone from, working in integers from the `Gdx.graphics` calls to working in floats from the `viewport` calls.

Just update the members of the `GameScreen` class to be floats rather than integers. Additionally, in the `checkAndPlaceApple()` method, we need to cast our maths to an int as the `MathUtils.random()` method will interpret them as floats and will not place our apple correctly anymore:

```
appleX = MathUtils.random((int) (viewport.getWorldWidth() / SNAKE_
MOVEMENT) - 1) * SNAKE_MOVEMENT;
appleY = MathUtils.random((int) (viewport.getWorldHeight() / SNAKE_
MOVEMENT) - 1) * SNAKE_MOVEMENT;
```

This will do the trick!

Finally, to ensure that our batch instance renders everything in our world, we need to update the project and also update the view of the cameras. So, update the `draw()` method with the following:

```
private void draw() {
    batch.setProjectionMatrix(camera.projection);
    batch.setTransformMatrix(camera.view);
    batch.begin();
    // Code ommited for brevity
}
```

While we are at it, we should do the same for our grid:

```
private void drawGrid() {
    shapeRenderer.setProjectionMatrix(camera.projection);
    shapeRenderer.setTransformMatrix(camera.view);
    shapeRenderer.begin(ShapeRenderer.ShapeType.Line);
    // Code omitted for brevity
}
```

Now when you run the game, regardless of the screen size, our game world will always be a 20 x 15 cell grid for our snake to slither around!

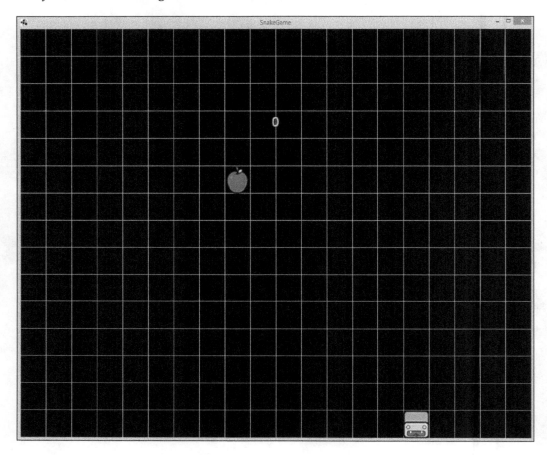

The preceding screenshot is taken at the same screen size as the previous screenshot but our game world is now consistent with our game.

I would like to end this topic with a suggestion. Go try out the other viewport classes; nothing bad will happen, but have a play with different viewports and different screen sizes so you get an idea of what each one does.

Summary

Well, that's the end of our Snake game. Over the course of this chapter, we took our humble Snake game from a very simple concept and fleshed it out with some game concepts, high scores, game states, and better collision handling. We had a chance to look at a couple of concepts that will make game development easier going forward: the ShapeRenderer class for debugging, and viewports for managing different screen sizes and allowing us to work in a consistent world.

In the next chapter, we will start building a game similar to the one that was a viral smash when it came out. Don't worry; it isn't something to get into a flap about. We will look at using LibGDX's Scene2D for easy UI development, spritesheets to compact our artwork, and screens to help break up our game.

4

What the Flap Is the Hype About?

Back in 2013, there was a game featuring a little bird that flapped onto the scene in a way only most indie games makers can dream of, that game was Flappy Bird. In this chapter, we are going to look at doing what most people did in 2014, make a Flappy Bird clone!

We will cover the following topics:

- Why Flappy Bird?
- The project setup
- Creating Flappee Bee
- Flapping Flappee Bee
- Flower power obstacles
- Textures and animations
- GUI creation with Scene2D
- The Start screen and disposal

Why Flappy Bird?

Flappy Bird has to be, perhaps, the best definition of an overnight success. So much so that the developers who made it ended up pulling it off the app stores as they couldn't handle the sudden coverage the game got. Luckily, for the addicted many, they put it back.

The premise of this game is, like Snake, straightforward. You just have to guide your character through an infinite series of gates, which are in different positions. To do this, you need to tap the screen. Tapping the screen causes the character to move upward. When you are not tapping, it will dive down. You gain a point for every gate you go through, and the game is over when your character collides with a gate.

Simple, yet it is excruciatingly difficult to play and do well. This was the main driver for the people who kept coming back.

The project setup

Ok, new game, new project. We will start with a blank canvas; so go through and create a project like we did in the previous example.

Using the LibGDX Project Generator, call the game `FlappeeBee` and give it a game class name of `FlappeeBeeGame`.

The package can be anything you like, and then set the destination to wherever you wish to keep your code. Finally, uncheck every checkbox except **Desktop**.

Once this is done, click on **Generate** and then import the project into your choice of IDE.

Setting up the GameScreen class

With this being a fresh project, hot off the generator. It will have the default Hello World! game inside. Just bear this in mind for the moment.

Next, we create our own `GameScreen` class. Remember, when you create this, we just need it to extend `ScreenAdaptor`:

```
public class GameScreen extends ScreenAdapter {
}
```

The preceding code is what you should have in your `GameScreen` class for now. So, next we need to populate it with a few things that you might recognize from the Snake game.

First, let's give the game a world to live in. As `FlappeeBee` will be a portrait game, we can just switch the values we used before:

```
private static final float WORLD_WIDTH = 480;
private static final float WORLD_HEIGHT = 640;
```

Add the preceding code to your `GameScreen` class.

Next, let's set up the objects that are going to be doing the heavy lifting of rendering and view handling:

```
private ShapeRenderer shapeRenderer;
private Viewport viewport;
private Camera camera;
private SpriteBatch batch;
```

Add the preceding members to the class, and then let's create the following methods as well:

```
@Override
public void resize(int width, int height) {
  viewport.update(width, height);
}

@Override
public void show() {
  camera = new OrthographicCamera();
  camera.position.set(WORLD_WIDTH / 2, WORLD_HEIGHT / 2, 0);
  camera.update();
  viewport = new FitViewport(WORLD_WIDTH, WORLD_HEIGHT, camera);
  shapeRenderer = new ShapeRenderer();
  batch = new SpriteBatch();
}

@Override
public void render(float delta) {
  clearScreen();
  batch.setProjectionMatrix(camera.projection);
  batch.setTransformMatrix(camera.view);
  batch.begin();
  batch.end();
}

private void clearScreen() {
  Gdx.gl.glClearColor(Color.BLACK.r, Color.BLACK.g,
  Color.BLACK.b, Color.BLACK.a);
  Gdx.gl.glClear(GL20.GL_COLOR_BUFFER_BIT);
}
```

Now, our `GameScreen` class is ready to rock and roll!

Our final setup task before we dive into making FlappeeBee is to update the `FlappeeBeeGame` class. If you remember how the `SnakeGame` class looked, this will look very familiar to you, especially as it makes the class very simple.

First, change the parent class to `Game` and then remove all the code from the body of the class and add the following code:

```
@Override
public void create() {
  setScreen(new GameScreen());
}
```

Excellent! With this added, we can now start! But before we go, I will just give a recap of what we have set up here.

Our `GameScreen` class uses the screens functionality in LibGDX to help make managing the lifecycle of a game easier along with logically splitting the game up.

The `Viewport` parameter helps with projecting our game world onto the screen of the player. The `Camera` parameter is maintained by the `Viewport` parameter and we use it to update the `SpriteBatch` parameter so that our world is projected and transformed correctly on to the players' screen. Finally, we have the `ShapeRenderer` class; this will be useful to debug our collisions and placeholders for our game objects before we use the art.

Creating Flappee Bee

So at this point, we should have a project set up and ready to go. I hope you have even tried to run it. It should have just shown a black screen, it's not a game yet!

Let's start by breaking this game down into its components so that we can implement them in a set of smaller steps. This won't be quite how it happens in real life as sometimes the game's rules might not have been set in stone and so there would be a chance things would change. However, since we know the game we want to make and the rules are set, let's do it!

Flappee Bee

The main character in our game is Flappee Bee, which tries to bumble its way through the flowers.

Let's pretend that we don't have the art on hand to start rendering old Flappee to the screen. Instead, let's use our `ShapeRenderer` to get things started so we can get the game playable.

First, let's create a class that will look after Flappee; it will contain properties that only apply to Flappee, along with the logic to manipulate the character. So, let's create that class called `Flappee`. Next, we will populate it with the following code:

```
public class Flappee {

    private static final float COLLISION_RADIUS = 24f;
    private final Circle collisionCircle;

    private float x = 0;
    private float y = 0;

    public Flappee() {
        collisionCircle = new Circle(x,y, COLLISION_RADIUS);
    }

    public void drawDebug(ShapeRenderer shapeRenderer) {
        shapeRenderer.circle(collisionCircle.x, collisionCircle.y,
        collisionCircle.radius);
    }
}
```

Now, we'll discuss what we have added here; first, we have defined a collision area for Flappee, in this instance, it is a circle.

Why did I pick a circle? I am sure you must be wondering. Well, for me, it is the one that best represents a real life bee – particularly the Bumble Bee. Now, I suppose you are wondering why I am using a radius of 24? Before I answer that, I will just quickly explain that the constructor I am using for the `Circle` class takes three properties: x, y, and the radius. As we don't know where Flappee will bee (read be) – I think I will be restricted to one pun per book at this rate – we can just set the x and y coordinates of the circle to be the default of (0,0). As for the radius, well being the author of this book, I know what is going to happen later and what the size of the art asset is that will use. So, for now the radius is arbitrary, but it won't be the same later. Trust me on this one.

Finally, we created a render method where we can pass `ShapeRenderer` in and draw our circle.

Now, we have Flappee; let's add him to the `GameScreen` class:

```
private Flappee flappee = new Flappee();
```

Then, update the `render()` method to draw Flappee:

```
public void render(float delta) {
  /* Other code omitted for brevity */
  shapeRenderer.setProjectionMatrix(camera.projection);
  shapeRenderer.setTransformMatrix(camera.view);
  shapeRenderer.begin(ShapeRenderer.ShapeType.Line);
  flappee.drawDebug(shapeRenderer);
  shapeRenderer.end();
}
```

Now, let's fire up the `desktop:run` task in this project and see what we get!

Oh! Before you do, we should update our `DesktopLauncher` class so we can specify a sensible screen size; 240 x 320 should suffice:

```
public class DesktopLauncher {
  public static void main (String[] arg) {
    LwjglApplicationConfiguration config = new
    LwjglApplicationConfiguration();
    config.height = 320;
    config.width = 240;
    new LwjglApplication(new FlappeeBeeGame(), config);
  }
}
```

Let's take a look at the following screenshot:

Well, that wasn't what we were expecting, was it?

Hands up who thought that the x and y coordinates were going to be at the bottom left of the circle and not the center? Now, hands up who read the JavaDoc and knew this was going to happen?

Well, to be honest, this doesn't affect us that much going forward. We will just have to remember this when it comes to rendering the texture over the top as we will need to offset the texture to compensate for this.

The next question we need to answer is, "where do we place Flappee on the screen?" Well, let's think about the gameplay here: the player taps the screen, the character flies up on tap, and down on no tap, and obstacles come along from the right. As what is commonly found in software development, there are several different ways to solve this problem. You can have the character fly through the world with the obstacles being static, or you can have the obstacles moving horizontally through the world and the character being static (in the horizontal plane at least).

Considering that we will want to randomly generate obstacles, I will say we go with the latter of these two ideas.

This means that Flappee will consistently be in the same x coordinate in the world space but the y coordinate will vary depending on the input. So, let's place him in an appropriate place.

Firstly, let's update our `Flappee` class so we can manipulate his starting position:

```
public void setPosition(float x, float y) {
  this.x = x;
  this.y = y;
  updateCollisionCircle();
  }

private void updateCollisionCircle() {
    collisionCircle.setX(x);
    collisionCircle.setY(y);
  }
```

What we are doing here is applying the given x and y values to the class members, and then updating our circle to match that position.

Next, add a method call to the `GameScreen` class:

```
public void show() {
    /** Code omitted for brevity **/
    flappee.setPosition(WORLD_WIDTH / 4, WORLD_HEIGHT / 2);
  }
```

Here, we set the position to be precisely a quarter of the width of our world area and half of the world height.

Let's run our project again and see what we get!:

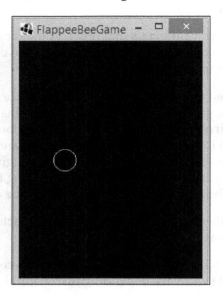

Much better! I can see this game coming together already! No? You don't? Ah OK, let's start making Flappee move.

Flapping Flappee

Our next step will be moving the character in an up and down motion. As we know, if there isn't any input, then Flappee will just fall down from its flight, and if we are true to the original, then it should be a pretty steep dive too!

We will need to add a couple of properties to our `Flappee` class to take the dive into consideration. We will need to know not only the speed that Flappee is subjected to, but also how quickly that speed should change, that is, the acceleration. Add the following code to our `Flappee` class:

```
private static final float DIVE_ACCEL = 0.30F;
private float ySpeed = 0;
```

So, here we have the acceleration `DIVE_ACCEL`, which is going to be the rate of change and `ySpeed`, which we will use to keep track of the speed—in this case on vertically.

Next, let's add an `update()` method that can be called:

```
public void update() {
  ySpeed -= DIVE_ACCEL;
  setPosition(x, y + ySpeed);
}
```

Here, we have our speed being updated and then applied to Flappee's position.

Finally, add a call to the `GameScreen` class:

```
public void render(float delta) {
  /* Code omitted for brevity */
  update(delta);
}

private void update(float delta) {
  flappee.update();
}
```

If you run the project now, you will see our white circle drop just out of view.

Our next task is to have Flappee fly up in response to some input from the player. What we will do is use the space bar for this task.

First, let's add the acceleration required for flying up in the `Flappee` class:

```
private static final float FLY_ACCEL = 5F;
```

I would like to point out that the values I used for the acceleration came from trial and error. Feel free, once we are done here, to go through and try different values!

Next, we need to create a method that will cause the manipulation upon input:

```
public void flyUp() {
  ySpeed = FLY_ACCEL;
  setPosition(x, y + ySpeed);
}
```

Here, we cancel any current speed and set it to our flying up acceleration, then we update Flappee's position.

Finally, in our `GameScreen` class, we need to add some input detection and call the `flyUp()` method. Let's update our `update()` method with the following:

```
private void update(float delta) {
  flappee.update();
  if (Gdx.input.isKeyPressed(Input.Keys.SPACE)) flappee.flyUp();
}
```

By pressing the spacebar, we call our `flyUp()` method.

Run the project and you can now try this out. Just watch out, Flappee will fly off the screen if you aren't careful!

In fact, let's sneak that code in now, as it will be useful later on!

Create the following method in our `GameScreen` class and add a call to the `update` method:

```
private void blockFlappeeLeavingTheWorld() {
  flappee.setPosition(flappee.getX(),
  MathUtils.clamp(flappee.getY(), 0, WORLD_HEIGHT));
}
private void update(float delta) {
  flappee.update();
  if (Gdx.input.isKeyPressed(Input.Keys.SPACE)) flappee.flyUp();
  blockFlappeeLeavingTheWorld();
}
```

Here, we use a handy method called `clamp()` from the LibGDX `MathUtils` class. This allows us to bound a value between a lower and an upper limit. This class has several useful methods, feel free to check out the JavaDoc on the LibGDX at http://libgdx.badlogicgames.com/nightlies/docs/api/com/badlogic/gdx/math/MathUtils.html for more information.

Now, our little circle won't go off screen.

Flower power obstacles

With Flappee going up and down, we now need to introduce some obstacles for him to avoid. From an artistic perspective, this is going to take the form of a flower, but in terms of our collision detection and shape rendering, it will take the form of something along the lines of a lollipop. However, you might be thinking there are two obstacles that come at once, one from the ceiling and one from the floor, and that's perfectly fine. All we will need to do is invert one to get the other. Let's start working on the one on the floor.

First, let's create a class that is going to be looking after this obstacle. Let's call it `Flower`; the make up of this class is going to be similar to the `Flappee` class, in that there will be collision areas, a way to set the position, a way to update the collision areas, and, of course, a debug render method. The following is the code listing for the `Flower` class:

```
public class Flower {

    private static final float COLLISION_RECTANGLE_WIDTH = 13f;
    private static final float COLLISION_RECTANGLE_HEIGHT = 447f;
    private static final float COLLISION_CIRCLE_RADIUS = 33f;
    private final Circle collisionCircle;
    private final Rectangle collisionRectangle;

    private float x = 0;
    private float y = 0;

    public Flower() {
        this.collisionRectangle = new Rectangle(x, y,
        COLLISION_RECTANGLE_WIDTH, COLLISION_RECTANGLE_HEIGHT);
        this.collisionCircle = new Circle(x + collisionRectangle.width
        / 2, y + collisionRectangle.height, COLLISION_CIRCLE_RADIUS);
    }

    public void setPosition(float x) {
        this.x = x;
        updateCollisionCircle();
        updateCollisionRectangle();
    }

    private void updateCollisionCircle() {
        collisionCircle.setX(x + collisionRectangle.width / 2);
    }

    private void updateCollisionRectangle() {
        collisionRectangle.setX(x);
    }

    public void drawDebug(ShapeRenderer shapeRenderer) {
        shapeRenderer.circle(collisionCircle.x, collisionCircle.y,
        collisionCircle.radius);
        shapeRenderer.rect(collisionRectangle.x, collisionRectangle.y,
        collisionRectangle.width, collisionRectangle.height);
    }
}
```

I am not going to go into too much detail of the class till now, as it is fairly self-explanatory and is similar to the `Flappee` class. The one thing I would like to point out is the positioning of the circle:

```
private void updateCollisionCircle() {
  collisionCircle.setX(x + collisionRectangle.width / 2);
  collisionCircle.setY(y + collisionRectangle.height);
}
```

As you can see from the preceding code snippet, we position the circle relative to the rectangle. This is done so that when it is placed on the screen, the circle will be at the top of the rectangle and centrally aligned.

If we quickly add the `Flower` class to the `GameScreen` class and draw it out, we get the following:

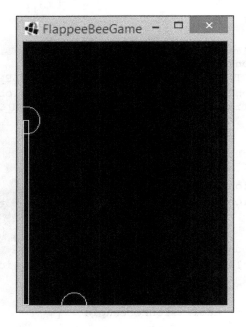

As you can see from the image, we get the shape we are looking, just positioned in a place where we don't want it. You might be wondering at this stage, "why is it so tall?" Well, if you recall, in the original game, the heights varied according to the obstacles. This is going to be pretty much the limit that we will allow the bottom obstacle to come up to.

Next, we need to start making it scroll across the screen.

Moving the obstacle is really just an act of updating the *x* position of the flower.

First, let's add a constant to define the speed at which we want our obstacle to move across the screen:

```
private static final float MAX_SPEED_PER_SECOND = 100F;
```

Then, let's create an `update()` method for the `Flower` class:

```
public void update(float delta) {
  setPosition(x - (MAX_SPEED_PER_SECOND * delta));
}
```

So, what we are saying here is that we want our flower to move across the screen at 100 world units a second. We achieve this by multiplying the given constant with a delta value we get from LibGDX. This delta value is the time since the last render of the screen, and given that we are running at 60 frames a second, it should be around the value of 0.016667.

Next, let's update our `GameScreen` class to allow for creating, updating, and removing our obstacles, or flowers, as they move across the screen.

First, we need to hold all the references we have to the `Flower` class, and we can do this using one of LibGDX's data types, the `Array` class:

```
private Array<Flower> flowers = new Array<Flower>();
```

Next, we are going to create a method to create our flowers for us, which is as follows:

```
private void createNewFlower() {
  Flower newFlower = new Flower();
  newFlower.setPosition(WORLD_WIDTH + Flower.WIDTH);
  flowers.add(newFlower);
}
```

Here, we have the `Flower` class being instantiated and then set to a position that is the `WORLD_WIDTH` value with the addition of the width of the flower, which in this case, is in the `Flower` class:

```
public static final float WIDTH = COLLISION_CIRCLE_RADIUS * 2;
```

We then add it to the array. We now need to decide a way to check whether we need to create a new `Flower` instance. There are two situations we need to consider when we need to create a new `Flower` instance. The first instance being that there aren't any flowers at all and the second if the last added `Flower` instance has crossed a certain threshold. This will allow us to have a consistent gap between our obstacles. We can do this with the following method:

```
private void checkIfNewFlowerIsNeeded() {
  if (flowers.size == 0) {
```

```
        createNewFlower();
    } else {
      Flower flower = flowers.peek();
      if (flower.getX() < WORLD_WIDTH - GAP_BETWEEN_FLOWERS) {
        createNewFlower();
      }
    }
}
```

So, as you can see, we are satisfying both criteria. If the array is empty, this means there are no obstacles - this will of course be the case at the start of the game. Otherwise if there are items in the array then we can go ahead and handle the obstacles. We do this by using the peek() method (this looks at the last added object) and we test the x position of the obstacle, if the position is less then our constant value—GAP_BETWEEN_FLOWERS—away from the right end edge of the world we add another obstacle to the array.

The GAP_BETWEEN_FLOWERS value in this case is:

```
private static final float GAP_BETWEEN_FLOWERS = 200F;
```

The number might sound arbitrary, but again, this is just from trial and error of what feels right; feel free to change this number to see a different effect!

The final part, before we get to the code to update our obstacles, is to check whether we want to remove the first one in the array, as this is the one that will be the furthest left. We do this as follows:

```
private void removeFlowersIfPassed() {
  if (flowers.size > 0) {
    Flower firstFlower = flowers.first();
    if (firstFlower.getX() < -Flower.WIDTH) {
      flowers.removeValue(firstFlower, true);
    }
  }
}
```

We check whether the array contains obstacles; if it does, get the first obstacle in the array and test the x position. Now, you might be wondering why we are using—FLOWER_WIDTH here as our comparison and not just 0, the left hand edge of the screen. If we set it to 0, then the flower will just disappear from view and would look a bit unconventional, as you would expect the flower to drift off to the left of and move out of your view. Additionally, -Flower.WIDTH is just shorthand for 0 - Flower.WIDTH.

Now, we have all the tools for our army of flower obstacles. We just need to package them together and have the obstacles rendered! The following code is in the GameScreen class:

```
private void update(float delta) {
  /* Code omitted for brevity */
  updateFlowers(delta);
}
private void updateFlowers(float delta) {
  for (Flower flower : flowers) {
    flower.update(delta);
  }
  checkIfNewFlowerIsNeeded();
  removeFlowersIfPassed();
}
private void drawDebug() {
  /* Code omitted for brevity */
  for (Flower flower : flowers) {
    flower.drawDebug(shapeRenderer);
  }
  /* Code omitted for brevity */
}
```

With all that in place, if we now run the project, you should hopefully see something similar to the following screenshot:

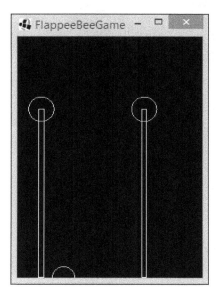

With the obstacles scrolling across the screen, if you start pressing the spacebar, you can almost make a game out of this.

Let's now turn our attention to varying the height of these obstacles. This is easily done by specifying a *y* value upon the creation of our flowers.

First, let's define our constant for the height offset in the `Flower` class:

```
private static final float HEIGHT_OFFSET = -400f;
```

Now in our constructor, let's set our *y* value:

```
public Flower() {
    this.y = MathUtils.random(HEIGHT_OFFSET);
    /** Code omitted for brevity **/
}
```

What we are saying here is that we want our y value to be a negative number between 0 and 400. This means our flower can either stand at 447 world units high or be as low down as 47. Again, I chose this number after some trial and error, feel free to play around and try something different.

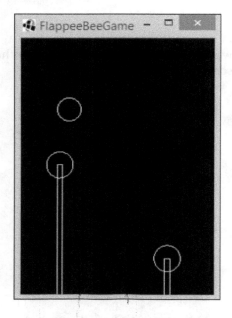

Hopefully, you now get something similar when you play the game!

The last task to do with our obstacles is to have an upside down obstacle coming from the ceiling. This can be tackled in multiple ways but we can use a simple approach of just reflecting the collision areas in the `Flower` class. We can start by adding the new collision areas, as shown in the following code:

```
private static final float DISTANCE_BETWEEN_FLOOR_AND_CEILING =
225F;
private final Circle floorCollisionCircle;
private final Rectangle floorCollisionRectangle;
private final Circle ceilingCollisionCircle;
private final Rectangle ceilingCollisionRectangle;
public Flower() {
  this.y = MathUtils.random(HEIGHT_OFFSET);
  this.floorCollisionRectangle = new Rectangle(x, y,
  COLLISION_RECTANGLE_WIDTH, COLLISION_RECTANGLE_HEIGHT);
  this.floorCollisionCircle = new Circle(x +
  floorCollisionRectangle.width / 2, y +
  floorCollisionRectangle.height, COLLISION_CIRCLE_RADIUS);

  this.ceilingCollisionRectangle = new Rectangle(x,
  floorCollisionCircle.y + DISTANCE_BETWEEN_FLOOR_AND_CEILING,
  COLLISION_RECTANGLE_WIDTH, COLLISION_RECTANGLE_HEIGHT);
  this.ceilingCollisionCircle = new Circle(x +
  ceilingCollisionRectangle.width / 2,
  ceilingCollisionRectangle.y, COLLISION_CIRCLE_RADIUS);
}
```

It should be noted here that I have changed the names of the existing collision zones to make it clear where they are.

So, here I added a constant—DISTANCE_BETWEEN_FLOOR_AND_CEILING. This will be the gap the player has to get Flappee through. Then, in the constructor, we create our new collision areas. This time, their positions are offset using the new constant and are relative to the position of the floor collision circle. The distance, again, is from trial and error.

We can now update the other methods in the `Flower` class to take these new collision areas into account:

```
private void updateCollisionCircle() {
  floorCollisionCircle.setX(x + floorCollisionRectangle.width /
  2);
  ceilingCollisionCircle.setX(x + ceilingCollisionRectangle.width
  / 2);
}

private void updateCollisionRectangle() {
```

```
    floorCollisionRectangle.setX(x);
    ceilingCollisionRectangle.setX(x);
}

public void drawDebug(ShapeRenderer shapeRenderer) {
    shapeRenderer.circle(floorCollisionCircle.x,
    floorCollisionCircle.y, floorCollisionCircle.radius);
    shapeRenderer.rect(floorCollisionRectangle.x,
    floorCollisionRectangle.y, floorCollisionRectangle.width,
    floorCollisionRectangle.height);
    shapeRenderer.circle(ceilingCollisionCircle.x,
    ceilingCollisionCircle.y, ceilingCollisionCircle.radius);
    shapeRenderer.rect(ceilingCollisionRectangle.x,
    ceilingCollisionRectangle.y, ceilingCollisionRectangle.width,
    ceilingCollisionRectangle.height);
}
```

When running our project, we should now have what almost resembles a skeleton version of our target game!

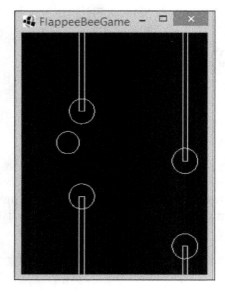

Collisions

Well, so far so good. However, we haven't implemented any collision handling. Luckily, LibGDX contains really useful tools to check for collision between the shapes that we are using. This is going to make our lives a lot easier.

The one class we will use is the `Intersector` class. To find out more, visit `http://libgdx.badlogicgames.com/nightlies/docs/api/com/badlogic/gdx/math/Intersector.html` and take a look at its API, you will see all sorts of useful methods there. However, we are only going to use two of them:

```
boolean overlaps(Circle c1, Circle c2)
boolean overlaps(Circle c, Rectangle r)
```

These will return `true` if the shapes overlap.

So, let's add a method to our `Flower` class that will take an instance of `Flappee` in and check the collision areas, as follows:

```
public boolean isFlappeeColliding(Flappee flappee) {
  Circle flappeeCollisionCircle = flappee.getCollisionCircle();
  return
  Intersector.overlaps(flappeeCollisionCircle,
  ceilingCollisionCircle) ||
  Intersector.overlaps(flappeeCollisionCircle,
  floorCollisionCircle) ||
  Intersector.overlaps(flappeeCollisionCircle,
  ceilingCollisionRectangle) ||
  Intersector.overlaps(flappeeCollisionCircle,
  floorCollisionRectangle);
}
```

This should also take place before adding the getter to the `Flappee` class; otherwise, this code will not compile. All we are doing here. What we are doing here, is checking the different collision areas and returning `true` if at least one of them overlapped.

Now, let's plug this into the `GameScreen` class. We can create a method to iterate the obstacles in play and check for collision, as follows:

```
private boolean checkForCollision() {
  for (Flower flower : flowers) {
    if (flower.isFlappeeColliding(flappee)) {
     return true;
    }
  }
  return false;
}
```

Then, in our `update()` method, we can check for the following code snippet:

```
private void update(float delta) {
  updateFlappee();
  updateFlowers(delta);
  if (checkForCollision()) {
    restart();
  }
}
```

I snuck a little `restart` method in there, which is as follows:

```
private void restart() {
  flappee.setPosition(WORLD_WIDTH / 4, WORLD_HEIGHT / 2);
  flowers.clear();
  score = 0;
}
```

So now, when Flappee collides with any of the obstacles, the game will—quite crudely, mind you—restart.

Scoring

Finally, to make this more game-like, we will need to add some scoring. The original game gave the player a point every time they cleared an obstacle, so let's do the same.

To do this, we need to consider a few things. First, we will need a way to identify whether the player has cleared an obstacle. Second, we need to ensure that we only reward the player once for each obstacle cleared; finally, how are we going to display the score to the player?

Let's tackle this first issue. We should award a point when the x coordinate of Flappee is greater than the x coordinate of the obstacle; remember, the obstacles move, Flappee does not. This, as it turns out, is quite straightforward; in our `GameScreen` class, let's add a property to look after the score:

```
private int score = 0;
```

Next, let's have a method to update the score, given the parameters we just discussed:

```
private void updateScore() {
  Flower flower = flowers.first();
  if (flower.getX() < flappee.getX()) {
    score++;
  }
}
```

Finally, add the following code snippet to our `update()` method:

```
private void update(float delta) {
  updateFlappee();
  updateFlowers(delta);
  updateScore();
  if (checkForCollision()) {
    restart();
  }
}
```

Now, when you play the game, a score will add up. However, it will add up quickly. As the obstacle passes Flappee, the game will still validate the `updateScore()` as Flappee is passing an obstacle. So the player will get multiple points for clearing the same obstacle! This is something we don't want to do. So, how do we go about solving this problem? One way is to add a flag to the obstacle to say we have claimed the point for it.

In our `Flower` class, let's add a Boolean flag:

```
private boolean pointClaimed = false;
```

Next, let's add some access methods:

```
public boolean isPointClaimed() {
  return pointClaimed;
}

public void markPointClaimed() {
  pointClaimed = true;
}
```

Now, let's update our `updateScore()` method in the `GameScreen` class:

```
private void updateScore() {
  Flower flower = flowers.first();
  if (flower.getX() < flappee.getX() && !flower.isPointClaimed())
  {
    flower.markPointClaimed();
    score++;
  }
}
```

Hooray! Now only a single point will be added to the player's score.

Finally, let's have the score shown on the screen. This is going to be fairly similar to what we did with the Snake game.

Let's add `BitmapFont` to our `GameScreen` class:

```
private BitmapFont bitmapFont;
private GlyphLayout glyphLayout;
public void show() {
  /** Code omitted for brevity **/
  bitmapFont = new BitmapFont();
  glyphLayout = new GlyphLayout();
}
```

Next, let's reuse the `drawScore()` method from our Snake game:

```
private void drawScore() {
  String scoreAsString = Integer.toString(score);
  glyphLayout.setText(bitmapFont, scoreAsString);
  bitmapFont.draw(batch, scoreAsString,) (viewport.getWorldWidth()
  - glyphLayout.width / 2, (4 * viewport.getWorldHeight() / 5) -
  glyphLayout.height / 2);
}
```

Finally, what we can do is extract the actual drawing code from the `render()` method into its own `draw()` method:

```
private void draw() {
    batch.setProjectionMatrix(camera.projection);
    batch.setTransformMatrix(camera.view);
    batch.begin();
    drawScore();
    batch.end();
}
```

Excellent! Let's run our project and see the results:

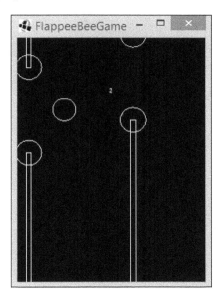

Perfect, a bit small on the font size. However, remember we are using the default font. Later on, we will explore using our fonts!

We now have a game; however, it is rather lacking in the art department. Luckily, our game artist has just delivered the assets for the game!

Here is a selection of the assets we will use!:

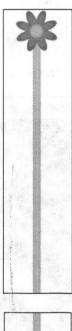

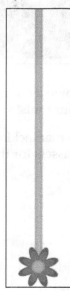

Adding textures and animations

We now have our assets. Let's add them to the assets folder in our project and start adding them into the game.

First up, let's add the background (bg.png). This is a relatively simple affair; like we did earlier, we create a Texture object that represents the background, then draw it. So, in the GameScreen class, add the following code:

```
private Texture background;

public void show() {
  /** Code omitted for brevity **/
  background = new Texture(Gdx.files.internal("bg.png"));
}

private void draw() {
  batch.setProjectionMatrix(camera.projection);
  batch.setTransformMatrix(camera.view);
  batch.begin();
  batch.draw(background, 0, 0);
  drawScore();
  batch.end();
}
```

Let's run it and see how it looks:

Excellent, we are almost there! OK, let's not kid ourselves, we still have more to do.

Next, let's bring those flowers to life.

First up, let's modify our `Flower` class to take two `Texture` objects, which will represent the top and bottom flowers. So, add the following code to your `Flower` class:

```
private final Texture floorTexture;
private final Texture ceilingTexture;

public Flower(Texture floorTexture,Texture ceilingTexture) {
  this.floorTexture = floorTexture;
  this.ceilingTexture = ceilingTexture;
  / ** Code omitted for brevity **/
}
```

Now, we need to render these, so let's create a `draw()` method:

```
public void draw(SpriteBatch batch) {
  batch.draw(floorTexture, floorCollisionRectangle.getX(),
  floorCollisionRectangle.getY());
  batch.draw(ceilingTexture, ceilingCollisionRectangle.getX(),
  ceilingCollisionRectangle.getY());
}
```

For the coordinates of the flower textures, we will use their corresponding collision rectangles' *x* and *y* values.

Next, let's update our `GameScreen` class. You might find that your IDE is now complaining about the `Flower` class, as we changed the constructor signature:

```
private Texture flowerBottom;
private Texture flowerTop;
public void show() {
  /** Code omitted for brevity **/
  flowerBottom = new
  Texture(Gdx.files.internal("flowerBottom.png"));
  flowerTop = new Texture(Gdx.files.internal("flowerTop.png"));
}
private void createNewFlower() {
  Flower newFlower = new Flower(flowerBottom, flowerTop);
  newFlower.setPosition(WORLD_WIDTH + Flower.WIDTH);
  flowers.add(newFlower);
}
```

So, here we define our textures and then pass them to our `Flower` class. Now we just need to add a call to our `draw()` method.

First, create a method called `drawFlowers()`. This will iterate over the `Flower` objects and call the `draw()` method for us:

```
private void drawFlowers() {
  for (Flower flower : flowers) {
    flower.draw(batch);
  }
}
```

Finally, add a call to this method in our main `draw()` method:

```
private void draw() {
  batch.setProjectionMatrix(camera.projection);
  batch.setTransformMatrix(camera.view);
  batch.begin();
  batch.draw(background, 0, 0);
  drawFlowers();
  drawScore();
  batch.end();
}
```

Good stuff! I think we should run our project and see what happens!

Oh! they are not where we were expecting them to be. This can be for a number of reasons, for instance, and in this case, our artist has added some padding around the texture for our flower. So, what we need to do is make the center of our flower texture relative to the center of the collision area.

Since we know that our collision circle's x value is the center of the collision area, we can use that as our reference point. Then, to get our texture's x value, we just subtract half the width of our texture from the collision circle's x value, as follows:

```
float textureX = floorCollisionCircle.x - floorTexture.getWidth()
/ 2;
```

Of course, it will still appear out of alignment on the y axis. To fix this we need adjust the position of the texture by our COLLISION_CIRCLE_RADIUS. So we can just add that value to our y as follows:

```
float textureY = floorCollisionRectangle.getY() +
COLLISION_CIRCLE_RADIUS;
```

Let's put all the preceding explanations together in a little method:

```
private void drawFloorFlower(SpriteBatch batch) {
    float textureX = floorCollisionCircle.x -
    floorTexture.getWidth() / 2;
    float textureY = floorCollisionRectangle.getY() +
    COLLISION_CIRCLE_RADIUS;
    batch.draw(floorTexture, textureX, textureY);
}
```

Now, update the draw() method:

```
public void draw(SpriteBatch batch) {
    drawFloorFlower(batch);
    batch.draw(ceilingTexture, ceilingCollisionRectangle.getX(),
    ceilingCollisionRectangle.getY());
}
```

Let's now run our project.

Perfect! Now, let's update the flower at the top by adding the following to your `Flower` class:

```
private void drawCeilingFlower(SpriteBatch batch) {
    float textureX = ceilingCollisionCircle.x -
    ceilingTexture.getWidth() / 2;
    float textureY = ceilingCollisionRectangle.getY() -
    COLLISION_CIRCLE_RADIUS;
    batch.draw(ceilingTexture, textureX, textureY);
}
```

At first glance, it might look like the same mathematics as the bottom flower, but the difference here is that we subtract the circle radius from the y position to move the image down.

Update the `Flower` `draw()` method again:

```
public void draw(SpriteBatch batch) {
    drawFloorFlower(batch);
    drawCeilingFlower(batch);
}
```

Again, let's run the project.

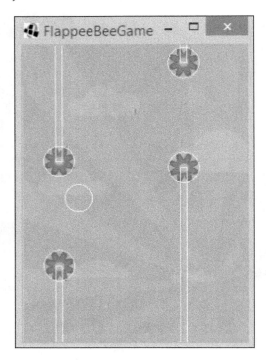

Spot on! Congratulate yourself. Just Flappee to bring to life now.

To bring Flappee to life, we go through a similar process to the one we did for the flowers. First, let's update our `Flappee` class:

```
private final Texture flappeeTexture;
public Flappee(Texture flappeeTexture) {
  this.flappeeTexture = flappeeTexture;
  /** Code omitted for brevity **/
}
public void draw(SpriteBatch batch) {
  batch.draw(flappeeTexture, collisionCircle.x,
  collisionCircle.y);
}
```

The astute among you might be asking why we are passing in our `Texture` object when we can get hold of a `FileHandle` instance statically and just create it in the constructor. Yes, you are correct, there is nothing to stop you from doing that. I have taken this approach, so that all our textures are created in the same place, that is, `GameScreen`, so it can be responsible for their life cycle, that is, dispose them when we no longer need them. You can handle the disposal in the `Flappee` class, but you might find that when stuff like this is hidden, it gets overlooked and before you know it, you are running out of memory because new textures keep getting created and are never disposed of.

Once again, we need to update our `GameScreen` class to reflect this change:

```
private Texture flappeeTexture;
public void show() {
  /** Code omitted for brevity **/
  flappeeTexture = new Texture(Gdx.files.internal("bee.png"));
  flappee = new Flappee(flappeeTexture);
  flappee.setPosition(WORLD_WIDTH / 4, WORLD_HEIGHT / 2);
}
private void draw() {
  batch.setProjectionMatrix(camera.projection);
  batch.setTransformMatrix(camera.view);
  batch.begin();
  batch.draw(background, 0, 0);
  drawFlowers();
  flappee.draw(batch);
  drawScore();
  batch.end();
}
```

In the preceding code listing, you will notice that we placed the construction of the `Flappee` object above the `setPosition()` method call. You might be aware that if we did this the other way around, we would get the dreaded `NullPointer` exception. Now, if we run our project, we will hopefully see a Flappee buzzing away on the screen!

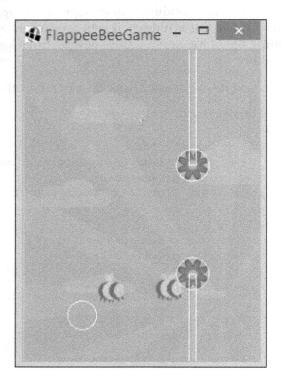

Oh no! First, he isn't where we expect him to be, and second, there are two! How did this happen?

Well, truthfully, I knew this was going to happen. Take a look at the `bee.png` image we used for our texture. It contains two bees, this will come in useful later on when we are looking at animating Flappee. But for now, we only want a single bee.

How do we do this? Well luckily, LibGDX's `TextureRegion` class comes with a `split()` method that will slice up our image into a two-dimensional array of `TextureRegions`. A `TextureRegion` class is exactly what it says it is, a region of a texture. If you look at the code (yey for open source software!) you will see it contains a reference to the parent texture and a set of coordinates of the region this object will cover.

So, we know what a `TextureRegion` is, but how do we implement it into our game? First, we need to know the size, in pixels, we want for each region. In the case of Flappee, it is 118x x 118px. Next, we need to take our `Texture` object and make it `TextureRegion`, so we can call `split()` and get our array of images.

Let's update our `Flappee` class:

```
private static final int TILE_WIDTH = 118;
private static final int TILE_HEIGHT = 118;

public Flappee(Texture flappeeTexture) {
    this.flappeeTexture = new
    TextureRegion(flappeeTexture).split(TILE_WIDTH,
    TILE_HEIGHT)[0][0];
    collisionCircle = new Circle(x, y, COLLISION_RADIUS);
}
```

We refer to the size of region we want with the `TILE` constants. It makes sense to refer to them as tiles, as that is essentially what we are doing, turning our texture into tiles. Then, we are specifying that we want the tile in the first column and first row.

Let's have a run and check the output.

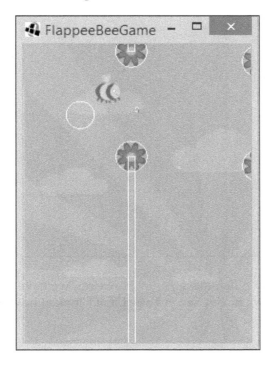

Almost there, let's now sort out that offset.

Similar to what we did in the `Flower` class, we center our texture relative to the center of the collision circle:

```
public void draw(SpriteBatch batch) {
    float textureX = collisionCircle.x -
    flappeeTexture.getRegionWidth() / 2;
    float textureY = collisionCircle.y -
    flappeeTexture.getRegionHeight() / 2;
    batch.draw(flappeeTexture, textureX, textureY);
}
```

Run it up and check it out! It should be bang on. Now for added effect, turn off the call to `drawDebug()` in the `GameScreen` class.

Now it is looking pretty much like a game! However, we have the opportunity to animate Flappee as we have a second asset. Let's look at how to make Flappee come to life.

Once again, LibGDX saves the day with a very useful class called `Animation`. An `Animation` class essentially holds an array of `TextureRegions` and, when given a set frame duration and a state timer, it can tell you which `TextureRegion` parameter to draw. It has a variety of different play modes as well:

- Normal
- Reversed
- Loop
- Loop reversed
- Loop pingpong
- Loop random

Visit the JavaDoc at `http://libgdx.badlogicgames.com/nightlies/docs/api/com/badlogic/gdx/graphics/g2d/Animation.PlayMode.html` for more information.

These modes affect how the `Animation` class decides which `TextureRegion` parameter should be shown.

Great! Let's get it into Flappee. First, we remove the old reference to `TextureRegion` that we had in the class and replace it with an `Animation` reference:

```
private final Animation animation;
```

Next, we update the constructor to instantiate the `Animation` class with an array of `TextureRegion` parameters:

```
public Flappee(Texture flappeeTexture) {
   TextureRegion[][] flappeeTextures = new
   TextureRegion(flappeeTexture).split(TILE_WIDTH, TILE_HEIGHT);

   animation = new Animation(FRAME_DURATION,flappeeTextures[0][0],
   flappeeTextures[0][1]);
   animation.setPlayMode(Animation.PlayMode.LOOP);

   collisionCircle = new Circle(x, y, COLLISION_RADIUS);
}
```

So, similar to what we did earlier, we split the textures and then pass in the references to the tile. In this case, it is row zero and columns zero and one. We also specify a `FRAME_DURATION` constant:

```
private static final float FRAME_DURATION = 0.25F;
```

Set PlayMode to LOOP.

Next, we add an animation timer:

```
private float animationTimer = 0;
```

We increment this value on every update call, so this means we need to update our update() method to do this:

```
public void update(float delta) {
   animationTimer += delta;
   ySpeed -= DIVE_ACCEL;
   setPosition(x, y + ySpeed);
}
```

Finally, we update our draw() method to access the Animation class and return the TextureRegion parameter we want to render:

```
public void draw(SpriteBatch batch) {
   TextureRegion flappeeTexture =
   animation.getKeyFrame(animationTimer);
   float textureX = collisionCircle.x -
   flappeeTexture.getRegionWidth() / 2;
   float textureY = collisionCircle.y -
   flappeeTexture.getRegionHeight() / 2;
   batch.draw(flappeeTexture, textureX, textureY);
}
```

Excellent, Flappee has been updated! However, we need to update our GameScreen class to reflect the change in our Flappee class:

```
private void update(float delta) {
   updateFlappee(delta);
   updateFlowers(delta);
   updateScore();
   if (checkForCollision()) {
     restart();
   }
}
private void updateFlappee(float delta) {
   flappee.update(delta);
   if (Gdx.input.isKeyPressed(Input.Keys.SPACE)) flappee.flyUp();
   blockFlappeeLeavingTheWorld();
}
```

Superb! We are now ready to run our project and see Flappee buzz!

GUI creation with Scene2D

We have our game, but you may be wondering why we haven't done anything with the lifecycle of the game, like we did with Snake. Well, that is because we are going to add new screens that will appear at the start and the end. But before we get on to creating and making the new screens, I want to talk about a really useful set of UI tools LibGDX offers for making UIs, Scene2D. Well, what is it?

According the LibGDX wiki page:

> *"Scene2d is a 2D scene graph for building applications and UIs using a hierarchy of actors."*

At its core, Scene2d is made of three classes:

- Actor: This contains the position, size (rectangular only), origin, scale, rotation, and color.
- Group: This is an Actor class that can contain other actors and children.
- Stage: This class has a Camera class, a SpriteBatch class, and a Group class. It orchestrates the updating, drawing, and input handling for all the children in its Group.

Of course, this wouldn't be LibGDX if it stopped there. There is a whole host of useful classes subclassed from the Actor classes.

Here is a link to the reference page for an Actor class: http://libgdx.badlogicgames.com/nightlies/docs/api/com/badlogic/gdx/scenes/scene2d/Actor.html.

I suggest that you take a look at the hierarchy so you can get a feel of how powerful Scene2d really is!

The Stage class

Let's have a quick chat about the Stage class before we get on to using it. A Stage class has two core methods that have to be called in order for it to work:

```
act(float delta);
draw();
```

The first method, act(), will go through and update all the child Actor classes in the graph. Each Actor has its own act() method, so it is this class that is called. It is useful to know this, as you may want to implement your own Actor implementation and you might want to do some specific work in every frame.

The second method, draw(), will render the UI graph to the screen. As you can imagine, this really simplifies the code of your game!

One last key thing to mention is that the Stage class is also an InputProcessor, this allows for it to fire off input events to the child Actor classes. This means that LibGDX needs to be told to use this class:

```
Gdx.input.setInputProcessor(stage);
```

It is really that simple to get up and running with Scene2d, however, more on that later. I would like to finish off telling you about the wonders of Scene2d.

The Actor class

An Actor class keeps track of all sorts of useful information about itself. A particular one I use often is the rotation of the Actor class. This is useful when it comes to rendering the Actor class as Scene2d automatically takes care of the rendering with rotation! The same applies to the scaling as well. This means we can focus more on making our game than building the UI.

The Actor classes also have a concept called Actions associated to them. An Action class is designed to manipulate the Actor class in some way, perhaps to move, scale, rotate, hide, or show it. The list goes on, you can build your own Action classes as well! As an added bonus, there is the ability to chain together a sequence of Action classes either in parallel or in a sequence. This gives us endless possibilities.

So what kind of Actors would we commonly use? Well, I can't speak for everyone who uses it but the classes you will find in my code are:

- Labels: These are used to display text
- ImageButtons/Buttons: This UI element has three states, namely normal, pressed, and checked

For more information on the Scene2d.ui components, check out LibGDX's wiki page at https://github.com/libgdx/libgdx/wiki/Scene2d.ui.

Finally, before we dive in and start making some UIs, this is just a small portion of what the Scene2d toolkit can do. We are just looking at the basics for now. We didn't cover, for example, the skinning or the styling aspects that can make the more complex UI easier to manage. With that said, let's crack on and make our new screens.

The Start screen and disposal

So, here we are back with Flappee Bee. The first thing we should tackle is having a Start screen, or menu screen, depending on what you want to call it. This `Screen` class will be built entirely with Scene2d.ui components and you will be mesmerized by how awesome all this is.

First things first; let's decide what we will have on our start screen. We will need a play button and some text, perhaps also a title image on the screen.

Let's create our `StartScreen` class and add the `Stage` classes to it:

```
public class StartScreen extends ScreenAdapter {

  private static final float WORLD_WIDTH = 480;
  private static final float WORLD_HEIGHT = 640;

  private Stage stage;

  public void show() {
    stage = new Stage(new FitViewport(WORLD_WIDTH, WORLD_HEIGHT));
    Gdx.input.setInputProcessor(stage);
  }

  public void resize(int width, int height) {
    stage.getViewport().update(width, height, true);
  }

  public void render(float delta) {
    stage.act(delta);
    stage.draw();
  }
}
```

As you can see, we are using concepts that should now be familiar to you - the use of the `Viewport` class and our world sizes. We tell LibGDX to use our `Stage` as the `InputProcessor`, we have our `Stage` instance call `act()` and `draw()`. I would say we are all set to add our first actor.

Our first actor is going to be the background image, this means we will use the `Image` class. To do this, we will need to create a reference to our background texture, then pass it to the `Image` class, and then add it to the `Stage` instance, as follows:

```
private Texture backgroundTexture;
public void show() {
  stage = new Stage(new FitViewport(WORLD_WIDTH, WORLD_HEIGHT));
```

```
Gdx.input.setInputProcessor(stage);

backgroundTexture = new Texture(Gdx.files.internal("bg.png"));
Image background = new Image(backgroundTexture);

stage.addActor(background);
}
```

Before we run our project, we will need to update our `FlappeeBeeGame` class to point to our new `Screen` class:

```
public void create() {
    setScreen(new StartScreen());
}
```

Excellent! Now let's fire it up and see what we get.

Hopefully, you would have just seen the background on its own, which is awesome. Now look back at the code. You haven't had to worry about the rendering code as all the stage has taken care of that.

Next, let's add a play button to the screen. To do this, we will use the `ImageButton` class. We have two images on hand for the play button; one when the button is in a normal state and one when it is pressed in. If you look at the code for the `ImageButton` class, you will see there is a constructor that looks like it was made just for us! Let's take a look at the following code:

```
public ImageButton (Drawable imageUp, Drawable imageDown)
```

Aha! You might be wondering why these `Drawable` classes are here, you were probably expecting the `Texture`/`TextureRegion` classes. Well, textures can come in a variety of different ways, so by LibGDX being done this way, they aren't tied to the `Texture` class.

Ok, so then, how do we use it? Well, it is pretty straightforward; let's update our `StartScreen` with the following code:

```
private Texture playTexture;
private Texture playPressTexture;
public void show() {
    /** Code omitted for brevity **/
    playTexture = new Texture(Gdx.files.internal("play.png"));
    playPressTexture = new
    Texture(Gdx.files.internal("playPress.png"));
```

```
ImageButton play = new ImageButton(new TextureRegionDrawable(new
TextureRegion(playTexture)), new TextureRegionDrawable(new
TextureRegion(playPressTexture)));
    stage.addActor(play);
}
```

Here, we create our textures, then we create `TextureRegionDrawables`, a `Drawable` subclass, to hold our textures in. We then instantiate the `ImageButton` class and add it to the stage.

Let's start the game and see how it looks!

Yay! Provided you see what I see, you should have the button there. Also, if you click on it, you will see that it switches the texture for use to the depressed texture. Looking pretty smart! Even if the placement is not where we want it to be yet.

Let's fix the positioning before we move on to adding the title. The `Actor` class has a really interesting method signature for setting a position. There is the standard:

```
public void setPosition (float x, float y)
```

This will position the actor relative to its bottom-left corner. However, there is also this method:

```
public void setPosition (float x, float y, int alignment)
```

This, with the added alignment parameter, allows us to change the anchor point from the bottom-left corner to somewhere else. Check out the `Align` class here to see the options:

```
public class Align {
   static public final int center = 1 << 0;
   static public final int top = 1 << 1;
   static public final int bottom = 1 << 2;
   static public final int left = 1 << 3;
   static public final int right = 1 << 4;

   static public final int topLeft = top | left;
   static public final int topRight = top | right;
   static public final int bottomLeft = bottom | left;
   static public final int bottomRight = bottom | right;
}
```

We will look at using the `center` alignment. Update our `StartScreen` class with the following code:

```
play.setPosition(WORLD_WIDTH / 2, WORLD_HEIGHT / 4, Align.center);
```

We can add it just after we instantiate the `ImageButton` class. So, what we are saying here is, place the button at the center of the width and a quarter of the way up the screen relative to the center point. If we didn't have this functionality, we would have to work it out ourselves, with something like the following code:

```
play.setPosition(WORLD_WIDTH / 2 - play.getWidth() / 2, WORLD_HEIGHT /
4 - play.getHeight() / 2);
```

But yay for less code now! Plus the less code means less chance of making mistakes.

I hope you can see by now, how easy it is to build a UI with the Scene2d toolkit. Admittedly, we have only added a single button, but it's a small step in the right direction.

Our final act for artwork on the screen is placing the title texture. So, going through the same process as earlier, with the background, we need to update our `StartScreen` class with a title texture and then add it to the stage:

```
private Texture titleTexture;
public void show() {
   /* Code omitted for brevity */
   titleTexture = new Texture(Gdx.files.internal("title.png"));
   Image title = new Image(titleTexture);
```

```
    title.setPosition(WORLD_WIDTH /2, 3 * WORLD_HEIGHT / 4,
    Align.center);
    stage.addActor(title);
}
```

Here, we are just placing it above the play button.

If we run the project, we should get the following output:

We are almost there! Now, we just need to hook up what to do when you tap the play button, as you are going to want to start the game.

To do this, we need to add a listener to the play button and react to when it is called. LibGDX has an interface called `EventListener` that is used throughout Scene2d to propagate the events through the graph. Now, we can just take this interface to create our own implementation, where we check for a mouse click and then react. However, thankfully, someone has already created a useful class that does the bulk of the heavy lifting!

It is the `ActorGestureListener` class, which contains lots of methods we can chose to override if we wish to react to them, as follows:

```
touchDown (InputEvent event, float x, float y, int pointer, int
button) {}

touchUp (InputEvent event, float x, float y, int pointer, int
button) {}

tap (InputEvent event, float x, float y, int count, int button) {}
boolean longPress (Actor actor, float x, float y) { return false;}

fling (InputEvent event, float velocityX, float velocityY, int
button) {}

pan (InputEvent event, float x, float y, float deltaX, float
deltaY) {}

zoom (InputEvent event, float initialDistance, float distance) {}

pinch (InputEvent event, Vector2 initialPointer1, Vector2
initialPointer2, Vector2 pointer1, Vector2 pointer2) {}
```

We are interested in the `tap` method. As we would like to do something when the user taps the button. To do this, we need to instantiate and override the method and then add this listener to the play button object, as follows:

```
play.addListener(new ActorGestureListener() {
  @Override
  public void tap(InputEvent event, float x, float y, int count,
  int button) {
    super.tap(event, x, y, count, button);
  }
});
```

Now, every time the button is tapped, that method will get called. We just now need to decide what we are going to do with it. This, thankfully, is a pretty simple answer, as we want to start the game!

To do this, we need to change the `Screen` object that the `Game` object currently has referenced. This means we will need access to the `Game` object in our code. Let's do this by adding it as a constructor parameter to our `StartScreen` class:

```
private final Game game;
public StartScreen(Game game) {
  this.game = game;
}
```

Next, let's update our `tap` method to change the screen:

```
public void tap(InputEvent event, float x, float y, int count, int
button) {
    super.tap(event, x, y, count, button);
    game.setScreen(new GameScreen());
}
```

Perfect. Finally, we need to update our `FlappyBeeGame` class to pass in a reference to itself:

```
public void create() {
    setScreen(new StartScreen(this));
}
```

Done!

Run the project and see what happens; tapping on **Play** will start the game.

We are not using Scene2D to its fullest potential, yet, you can see how easy it is to create a UI that is simple and clear code it; just imagine if we had to do all that by hand!

The dispose() method

Before we close this chapter, I want to quickly show you how to dispose of your assets in an appropriate manner. We haven't done this so far as we have been continually using our textures throughout the life of the game. However, here we have a that a player will see, then go into the game, and probably never see this screen again in this instance of the game. This means we are giving away vital memory allocation to textures that can be freed up! Also, our `Stage` instance needs to clean up after itself.

Doing this is pretty basic stuff, so we should add it now. In our `StartScreen` class, let's override the `dispose()` method and call `dispose` on everything we wish to clear:

```
@Override
public void dispose() {
    stage.dispose();
    backgroundTexture.dispose();
    playTexture.dispose();
    playPressTexture.dispose();
    titleTexture.dispose();
}
```

As you can see, all the textures and the stage are disposed of. Next, since `dispose` isn't called for us automatically, we need to explicitly say when we want to clear up. Luckily, we know when this will happen—when we switch screens, of course! Let's take a look at the following code snippet:

```
play.addListener(new ActorGestureListener() {
  @Override
  public void tap(InputEvent event, float x, float y, int count,
  int button) {
    super.tap(event, x, y, count, button);
    game.setScreen(new GameScreen());
    dispose();
  }
});
```

Excellent. With what we are doing, the impact will be small; however, it is a good practice to get into the habit of cleaning up after yourself, as when you get on to making bigger and more demanding games—this could be a time saver!

Summary

Well, that was an epic chapter. Hopefully, by now, you are getting to grips with creating a game in LibGDX. In this chapter, we made a Flappy Bird clone—Flappee Bee. We looked at animations and implemented them for the main character. We were also introduced to the Scene2d toolkit, which we used to create a GUI for a start screen. Finally, we ended with a look at disposing of memory-based assets that are no longer in use, ensuring that our games are as memory-efficient as possible.

Coming up in the next chapter, we will take Flappee Bee further. We will look at the `AssetManager` and see how it can make our lives easier with regards to our texture handling. Also, in conjunction with that, we will create a `LoadingScreen` class. You will also learn about packing your assets into a single texture to perform better. Finally, we will look at using our own fonts in the game.

5
Making Your Bird More Flightworthy

Flappee Bee is flying pretty fine now, don't you think? However, we are still not done! This chapter will focus a bit more on the tools available to us in **LibGDX**. We will take a look at the `AssetManager` class and see how it can be used to make our life better. We will then use it to create a loading screen so that we can load our textures and at the same time provide feedback to the user that the game is doing something. We will then take this a step further and look at how we can combine our assets into a single entity and explain why this is a good habit to get into. Finally, we will look at Hiero, the font converter, which is built into LibGDX to allow us to convert and style fonts as we desire.

The following topics will be covered in this chapter:

- Loading assets asynchronously with the `AssetManager` class
- Creating a loading screen
- Using a texture packer to combine all the assets into a single texture
- Hiero — the LibGDX font converter

Let's load up them assets!

So, what is this `AssetManager` class that we want to take a look at? Well, according to the documentation what it does is:

 Loads and stores assets such as textures, bitmap fonts, tile maps, sounds, music, and so on. Visit the following link for more details: `http://libgdx.badlogicgames.com/nightlies/docs/api/com/badlogic/gdx/assets/AssetManager.html`

You might be wondering what it can do for us. Well, truthfully, it won't actually make an impact on the game we have here. The amount of assets we have isn't that large in number or size. So then, why are we looking at it? Because, later down the line, when you make your own awesome, amazing games, you will need to know about tools like this that will make your life easier!

Right now, Flappee Bee only has about seven textures with the biggest being the background which is 480 x 640 pixels in size. Having this amount of textures, of this size isn't going to cause us that much of a problem. However, what if we suddenly have lots of textures—equally not as good, but we will cover that later—or our textures are at a higher resolution? The second one is more likely to occur; my artist loves HD textures!

You might now be wondering what the impact would be if you were to have lots of large separate textures, and you are right to think this. Right now, with our textures being small and not as numerous they are loaded without delay. However, the moment they become bigger, they will appear to pause the game to the player. In Flappee Bee's case, it will be as the user presses the **Start** button; if our textures were huge, it would appear to the player the game had crashed as the hardware was loading the texture. While we can't completely negate this pause by using the `AssetManager` class, as certain assets will need to be loaded on the rendering thread, we can provide feedback to on the loading player the progress.

Just to reiterate at this stage, Flappee Bee probably doesn't need this `AssetManager` parameter as the resource loading is negligible at this stage. However, I see this as a great opportunity to use it as we can look at it in the most simple case. Most of the time, it will be your decision as a game-maker whether you want to use it. According to the LibGDX wiki page, the reasons why you would want to use the `AssetManager` parameter are as follows:

- Loading of most resources is done asynchronously, so you can display a reactive loading screen while things load.
- Assets are reference counted. If two assets, A and B, both depend on another asset C, C won't be disposed until A and B have been disposed. This also means that if you load an asset multiple times, it will actually be shared and only take up one lot of memory!
- It is a single place to store all your assets.
- It allows you to transparently implement things such as caches.

Personally, I always start all my games with the `AssetManager` parameter enabled! But like I said, I know what my artist is going want to provide me with.

Before we start using `AssetManager`, it might be worth just checking out the wiki page on the LibGDX website: `https://github.com/libgdx/libgdx/wiki/Managing-your-assets`

This will give you a better idea of what else it can do, as here, we are just going to focus on loading the textures.

Implementing the AssetManager parameter

Now, enough talk, lets code! In Flappee Bee, we currently have four textures that are used:

- `bg.png`
- `flowerBottom.png`
- `flowerTop.png`
- `bee.png`

We will load these textures and keep them around forever. However, if we were to have the game reload the `GameScreen` class at any point, the textures would be reloaded afresh, and since we are not disposing of the previous textures, we would just fill up the memory. The `AssetManager` parameter will ensure that we don't do that!

First things first, we need to add our `AssetManager` to our `GameScreen` class, and add the following to the `GameScreen` class:

```
private final AssetManager assetManager = new AssetManager();
public GameScreen() {
  assetManager.load("bg.png", Texture.class);
  assetManager.load("flowerBottom.png", Texture.class);
  assetManager.load("flowerTop.png", Texture.class);
  assetManager.load("bee.png", Texture.class);
  assetManager.finishLoading();
}
```

In the preceding code, we have instantiated the `AssetManager` then we have instructed which assets to load and their type. In this case, these are just of type `Texture`. Finally, we round it off by telling the manager to pause until it finishes loading. As certain aspects of the texture loading are done asynchronously and others are done synchronously, if we don't add the call to the `finishLoading()` method, then there is a chance we will crash our game when it tries to access something that doesn't exist. Right now, this would still cause a pause in our rendering, but let's finish adding the `AssetManager` and then look at rectifying it.

Next, we need to change the way we access the textures. Let's update the code in our `show()` method to reflect the new way:

```
public void show(){
    // Code omitted for brevity
    background = assetManager.get("bg.png");
    flowerBottom = assetManager.get("flowerBottom.png");
    flowerTop = assetManager.get("flowerTop.png");
    flappeeTexture = assetManager.get("bee.png");
    // Code omitted for brevity
}
```

Here, we no longer control the `Texture` object; we don't even know how the loading is handled, which from a software development perspective, is great—decoupled code!

We use the `get()` method to return our `Texture` parameter. If you now load the game, it will run just like it did earlier, except now we are using the power of the `AssetManager`.

If you would like to see what the `AssetManager` is loading, there is a logger available that we can set the log level to. Add the following code to the `GameScreen` constructor:

```
assetManager.getLogger().setLevel(Logger.DEBUG);
```

Now, when you run the preceding code, you will see the following output trace:

```
AssetManager: Loading: bg.png, com.badlogic.gdx.graphics.Texture
AssetManager: Loading: flowerBottom.png, com.badlogic.gdx.graphics.
Texture
AssetManager: Loading: flowerTop.png, com.badlogic.gdx.graphics.
Texture
AssetManager: Loading: bee.png, com.badlogic.gdx.graphics.Texture
```

Perfect!

Loading the loading screen!

Great! We now have the manager in place; however, you might argue that we are still in the same situation. If our textures were a lot larger or if we had many more, we would still get a pause.

So what can we do about this? Add a loading screen, of course!

Having a loading screen is a great way to provide information back to the player that the game is actually doing something rather than giving the appearance that the game has just crashed.

First, let's create a new `Screen` subclass, called `LoadingScreen`. This class will take a `FlappeeBeeGame` object in the constructor as we move the `AssetManager` object to the `FlappeeBeeGame` class, so we will have only one instance of this class.

Our `LoadingScreen` class should look something like this:

```java
public class LoadingScreen extends ScreenAdapter{

    private static final float WORLD_WIDTH = 480;
    private static final float WORLD_HEIGHT = 640;
    private static final float PROGRESS_BAR_WIDTH = 100;
    private static final float PROGRESS_BAR_HEIGHT = 25;
    private ShapeRenderer shapeRenderer;
    private Viewport viewport;
    private Camera camera;
    private float progress = 0;
    private final FlappeeBeeGame flappeeBeeGame;
    public LoadingScreen(FlappeeBeeGame flappeeBeeGame) {
        this.flappeeBeeGame = flappeeBeeGame;
    }

    @Override
    public void resize(int width, int height) {
        viewport.update(width, height);
    }

    @Override
    public void show() {
        camera = new OrthographicCamera();
        camera.position.set(WORLD_WIDTH / 2, WORLD_HEIGHT / 2, 0);
        camera.update();
        viewport = new FitViewport(WORLD_WIDTH, WORLD_HEIGHT, camera);
        shapeRenderer = new ShapeRenderer();
        flappeeBeeGame.getAssetManager().load("bg.png",
        Texture.class);
        flappeeBeeGame.getAssetManager().load("flowerBottom.png",
        Texture.class);
        flappeeBeeGame.getAssetManager().load("flowerTop.png",
        Texture.class);
        flappeeBeeGame.getAssetManager().load("bee.png",
        Texture.class);
    }

    @Override
    public void render(float delta) {
```

```
      update();
      clearScreen();
      draw();
   }

   @Override
   public void dispose() {
      shapeRenderer.dispose();
   }

   private void update() {
      if (flappeeBeeGame.getAssetManager().update()) {
         flappeeBeeGame.setScreen(new GameScreen());
      } else {
         progress = flappeeBeeGame.getAssetManager().getProgress();
      }
   }

   private void clearScreen() {
      Gdx.gl.glClearColor(Color.BLACK.r, Color.BLACK.g,
      Color.BLACK.b, Color.BLACK.a);
      Gdx.gl.glClear(GL20.GL_COLOR_BUFFER_BIT);
   }

   private void draw() {
      shapeRenderer.setProjectionMatrix(camera.projection);
      shapeRenderer.setTransformMatrix(camera.view);
      shapeRenderer.begin(ShapeRenderer.ShapeType.Filled);
      shapeRenderer.setColor(Color.WHITE);
      shapeRenderer.rect(
         (WORLD_WIDTH  - PROGRESS_BAR_WIDTH) / 2, (WORLD_HEIGHT  -
         PROGRESS_BAR_HEIGHT / 2),
         progress * PROGRESS_BAR_WIDTH, PROGRESS_BAR_HEIGHT);
      shapeRenderer.end();
   }
}
```

Let's break down what we have here. Some of it will be fairly familiar to what we have done earlier with the `Camera`, `Viewport`, and `ShapeRenderer` classes. The key point in this class is that we specify which textures to load in the `show()` method, as shown here. It should be noted that we have moved the `AssetManager` parameter from the `GameScreen` parameter to the `FlappeeBeeGame` class and added a simple getter:

```
public void show(){
   // Code omitted for brevity
```

```
flappeeBeeGame.getAssetManager().load("bg.png", Texture.class);
flappeeBeeGame.getAssetManager().load("flowerBottom.png",
Texture.class);
flappeeBeeGame.getAssetManager().load("flowerTop.png",
Texture.class);
flappeeBeeGame.getAssetManager().load("bee.png", Texture.class);
}
```

Next, in our `update()` method, we add the following code:

```
private void update() {
    if (flappeeBeeGame.getAssetManager().update()) {
        flappeeBeeGame.setScreen(new GameScreen());
    } else {
        progress = flappeeBeeGame.getAssetManager().getProgress();
    }
}
```

In the preceding code, you can see that we call the `update()` method on the `AssetManager` class this will give us an indication of whether or not it has finished loading. The manager will return `true` if it is complete, or `false` otherwise. If it is `false`, and there are more assets for the manager to load, we then query how far along the manager is and store this in a class level field for use later on. If the manager has completed all the asset loading, we can just change the screen to our game screen; job done!

Finally, we just need to give the player some sort of visual representation of the loading screen. There are many different ways this can be achieved; I am sure you have seen many yourself. Here, we will go with a traditional loading bar, but you may try out other ways in the future. Just remember, the more visually complex your loading screen becomes, the more it might need to be loaded itself!

Here is the code that handles the rendering of our progress bar:

```
private void draw() {
    shapeRenderer.setProjectionMatrix(camera.projection);
    shapeRenderer.setTransformMatrix(camera.view);
    shapeRenderer.begin(ShapeRenderer.ShapeType.Filled);
    shapeRenderer.setColor(Color.WHITE);
    shapeRenderer.rect(
        (WORLD_WIDTH  PROGRESS_BAR_WIDTH) / 2, (WORLD_HEIGHT -
        PROGRESS_BAR_HEIGHT) / 2,
    progress * PROGRESS_BAR_WIDTH, PROGRESS_BAR_HEIGHT);
    shapeRenderer.end();
}
```

The key piece of code is the `shaperenderer.rect()` call. We ask the renderer to draw a filled rectangle in the center of the screen, offset by its maximum sizes. We then calculate the width of the bar in proportion to the loading time. This will expand the progress bar as more and more assets are loaded.

We now have a loading screen; we just need to hook it to our screen flow. In our `StartScreen` parameter we can now update the **Play** button listener to set the screen to an instance of `LoadingScreen`, as shown here. It should be noted that the game class that we now have in `StartScreen` should be updated to the type `FlappyBeeGame`:

```
play.addListener(new ActorGestureListener() {
  @Override
  public void tap(InputEvent event, float x, float y, int count,
  int button) {
    super.tap(event, x, y, count, button);
    game.setScreen(new LoadingScreen(game));
    dispose();
  }
});
```

If you now launch the game, when you click on **Start**, you should get the loading screen briefly appearing before going to the actual game!

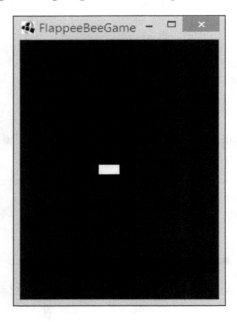

I agree it isn't much to look at, but it does the job!

To finish off, we can now remove the `AssetManager` object from the `GameScreen` parameter and just reference the one from the `FlappeeBeeGame` class.

So, update the `GameScreen` so that we now pass in the `FlappeeBeeGame` object, and then remove the `AssetManager` code we introduced previously. Now, update the `show()` method to reference the `FlappeeBeeGame` object, as follows:

```
public void show(){
  // Code omitted for brevity
  background = flappeeBeeGame.getAssetManager().get("bg.png");
  flowerBottom =
  flappeeBeeGame.getAssetManager().get("flowerBottom.png");
  flowerTop =
  flappeeBeeGame.getAssetManager().get("flowerTop.png");
  flappeeTexture =
  flappeeBeeGame.getAssetManager().get("bee.png");
  // Code omitted for brevity
}
```

Now, we will use the textures loaded while this screen is being loaded.

Going forward, there is much more you can do with the loading screen than we have done here; make it more dynamic with what it loads. Currently, it is very much tied to the game we have here. If we had multiple screens with different assets associated with them, it would get quite messy to do it all in one loading screen like we did here. However, you wouldn't want to load everything at once; essentially, we should only be loading what we need.

Packing textures

Currently, we have our textures as individual files. For a game the size of Flappee Bee, that would normally be OK, since during the game we have four files. However, what would happen if we started adding more and more in-game textures? Eventually, we would start slowing down the game. The reason for this is that the underlying OpenGL is performing something called a **bind** for every different texture it renders. Binding is relatively expensive. To combat this, we can combine our assets into a single sheet, ah! You might be thinking, "But now I have to know where in the sheet the image is?", "What pixels to cut out?", and "What if they are rotated or white-space trimmed to save space in the image?" Well, fear not; LibGDX has a tool for this that will save us time — `TexturePacker`.

Here is a link to the LibGDX wiki that will let you look deeper into the Texture Packer tool:

`https://github.com/libgdx/libgdx/wiki/Texture-packer`

However, before we do this, let me first show you how we can measure the impact of switching to a single sheet, or **texture atlas** as it is known.

Measuring the impact

We use a class called `SpriteBatch`, which keeps track of something that is called a render call. A render call occurs when the batch flushes out the vertices to the mesh; this will happen in a number of scenarios but the one we are interested in is when a texture that is being rendered changes.

Let's measure this, but only after looking at the render calls made in a frame before and after the change to a texture atlas. We can achieve this by accessing the `totalRenderCalls` field on the `SpriteBatch` object before and after we draw. To do so, let's update our `GameScreen` class to do this, with the following code:

```
private void draw(){
  batch.totalRenderCalls = 0;
  batch.setProjectionMatrix(camera.projection);
  batch.setTransformMatrix(camera.view);
  batch.begin();
  batch.draw(background, 0, 0);
  drawFlowers();
  flappee.draw(batch);
  drawScore();
  batch.end();
  Gdx.app.log("Debug", batch.totalRenderCalls);
}
```

In the preceding code, we reset the `totalRenderCalls` parameter before the rendering took place, and we just printed out the field's value once the render happened. I don't recommend this for production use, as this would occur on every frame, but here, it will be just fine for now. In fact, it would be a good time to mention the LibGDX logging; like the majority of logging tools out there, it is fairly simple to use. You can find more information on the logging tools in the following wiki:

`https://github.com/libgdx/libgdx/wiki/Logging`

Once you amend the `draw()` method, run the game and, hopefully, you will have the same amount of draw calls as I do here, which is five.

You are probably thinking, "Well, five isn't so bad." To an extent you are right, how we have it now isn't affecting the game—that's the important part here. However, if you don't keep track of something like this, you might start finding the performance slows down when the draw calls start incrementing as you add more visual components.

With that out of the way, let's load the `TexturePacker` tool.

The GDX-tools TexturePacker

First things first, we need to add the LibGDX tools dependency to our project so we can access the awesome tools that they provide.

In your `build.gradle` file for the project, update the desktop project entry with the tools dependency:

```
project(":desktop") {
  apply plugin: "java"
  dependencies {
    compile project(":core")
    compile "com.badlogicgames.gdx:gdx-tools:$gdxVersion"
    compile "com.badlogicgames.gdx:gdx-backend-lwjgl:$gdxVersion"
    compile "com.badlogicgames.gdx:gdx-
    platform:$gdxVersion:natives-desktop"
  }
}
```

If you refresh the Gradle project, it will download the dependency and the project will appear in your dependency list.

To run the `TexturePacker` parameter, we can either call it from the command line or we can do it in code. Let's take the code route for now, as it will have an added benefit later on.

As the `gdx-tools` module is now a dependency of the desktop module, we can update our `DesktopLauncher` class with the following lines of code:

```
public class DesktopLauncher {
  public static void main(String[] arg) throws Exception {
    LwjglApplicationConfiguration config = new
    LwjglApplicationConfiguration();
    config.height = 320;
    config.width = 240;
    TexturePacker.process("../assets", "../assets",
    "flappee_bee_assets");
    new LwjglApplication(new FlappeeBeeGame(), config);
  }
}
```

In the preceding code, we tell the `TexturePacker` parameter to run before the game launches, and specify the input and output directories and the name we want to give our atlas. There is another method `signature()` which allows for a Settings object to be passed, but we can use the defaults for now.

If you now run the game, you might not notice anything different, but once the game has launched, you will see that two files, `flappee_bee_assets.png` and `flappee_bee_assets.atlas`, have appeared in the `assets` directory of the core module.

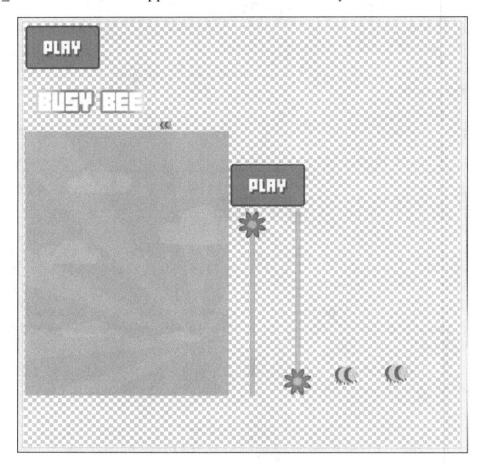

As we can see in this image, it has taken all the images and placed them into one image, our texture atlas!

Now, when you make your own games, you may decide to leave that texture packing code in place, so when you update your assets, they will automatically get packed for you when you run your desktop build.

Using the texture atlas

With our atlas generated, we can move on to using it. But before we do, I just want to tell you about the other atlas file that was generated, `flappee_bee_assets.atlas`. If you open the file, you will see that it is a text-based document that describes our atlas, pixel positions, rotations, and so on. This is how LibGDX will know where to get our textures from when we ask for them.

Our first port of call with updating the game to use the texture atlas is to change the `LoadingScreen` class to load the atlas instead of the other assets. We simply switch out the four calls to the `load()` method with one for the texture atlas, as follows:

```
public void show() {
   super.show();
   camera = new OrthographicCamera();
   camera.position.set(WORLD_WIDTH / 2, WORLD_HEIGHT / 2, 0);
   camera.update();
   viewport = new FitViewport(WORLD_WIDTH, WORLD_HEIGHT, camera);
   shapeRenderer = new ShapeRenderer();
   flappeeBeeGame.getAssetManager().load
   ("flappee_bee_assets.atlas", TextureAtlas.class);
}
```

In the long run, this will make our code cleaner as we have to reference fewer assets!

Next, we need to update our `GameScreen` class to reference the `TextureAtlas` class, and then assign the regions.

First, we need to switch from using the texture classes to the `TextureRegion` class:

```
private TextureRegion background;
private TextureRegion flowerBottom;
private TextureRegion flowerTop;
private TextureRegion flappeeTexture;
```

Then, we update it to reference the `TextureAtlas` class, in our `show()` method:

```
TextureAtlas textureAtlas = flappeeBeeGame.getAssetManager().
get("flappee_bee_assets.atlas");
background = textureAtlas.findRegion("bg");
flowerBottom = textureAtlas.findRegion("flowerBottom");
flowerTop = textureAtlas.findRegion("flowerTop");
flappeeTexture = textureAtlas.findRegion("bee");
```

As you can see in the preceding code, we pull out the texture atlas from the asset manager and locate the regions by their name. In this case, it is the filename minus the file extension.

Finally, you will need to update the `flappee` and `flower` classes to use `TextureRegion`, not texture.

Once this is complete, launch the game and you will hopefully see that the game is working the same as earlier, but the number of draw calls being traced out should have reduced down to two! It may not seem like it, but we have just massively reduced the amount of work the game has to do to render images to the screen. As we discussed at the beginning, you won't really notice the difference with Flappee Bee, but when you have a game with hundreds of textures, texture atlases really become your friends!

I need a Hiero!

In the final topic of this chapter, we will address fonts and their usage. So far in our game, we have used the default font in LibGDX, which is Arial size 15. While this is good for getting started, it isn't something that you would necessarily want in your final game. As you can see so far, one of the limitations is that it is too small!

So what can we do? Well, we can use our own fonts of course.

Let's start off by picking your favorite font; I found a font from a free site. There are plenty around, just do an Internet search and find a font you wish to use.

What you might find is that the font is in what's called a True Type font and this is usually denoted by the filename having the extension `.ttf` — .LibGDX does provide extensions to the library that will allow us to load this. However, for this exercise, I would like to introduce you to another tool in the LibGDX armory that I have used a lot.

That tool is Hiero.

What is Hiero?

Hiero is a bitmap font packing tool. It saves in the Angel Code font format, which can be used by `BitmapFont` in LibGDX applications:

`https://github.com/libgdx/libgdx/wiki/Hiero`

Hiero is a great little tool that rasterizes TTF fonts and allows various effects to be applied, such as a drop, shadow, or an outline.

Let's dive in and start using it. You will find the Hiero class in the `gdx-tools` module under the `com.badlogic.gdx.hiero` package. You should be able to run the `main()` method of the Hiero class; if it asks for a module, select Desktop. It will then load and you will be presented with this screen:

It is a fairly straightforward tool to use; you load the font you want, pick the desired size, specify the characters you wish to use, add an effect or two, and then save the output.

First, load your font or pick a system font. This should then appear in the **Rendering** box. We can keep size **32** for now, but we can revisit this if the font output is too small for our game.

Next, in the **Sample Text** screen, let's update this with the characters — or glyphs — we plan to use. Since we are going to use this to represent our score, we can update this to just contain **1234567890**.

Now, select **Glyph Cache**; some additional options will appear, these control the texture output of Hiero. If you adjust the page width and page height, you will notice that the Rendering window will update. We should aim to select a size so all the characters fit in the Rendering window, with minimal wasted space. By doing this we will reduce the final texture size.

Finally, the fun part—we can now add some effects. I am going to add just a simple outline to my font, but you can go wild and try different combinations and see what you get. It's OK, I will wait for you.

Done? Excellent.

Now, we just have to export the font. Select **Save** from the file drop-down menu and save the font file to the `assets` directory of our game (it is in the code module, remember?), giving the file a name of `score.fnt`—without the quotes.

With that done, if you look in the assets directory, you will see that two files have appeared: `score.fnt` and `score.png`. If you open `score.png`, you will notice that it is what we saw in Hiero's rendering box. If you open the `score.fnt` file, you will notice that it is essentially a mapping of characters to position in the `score.png` image.

Excellent! We should now be ready to go and use our font over the LibGDX default. A quick way to do this is to update the `GameScreen` class by updating the `BitmapFont` creation to pass in the new font, as follows:

```
bitmapFont = new BitmapFont(Gdx.files.internal("score.fnt"));
```

If you do what is given, then it will work. However, the quick thinkers among you will have realized that we just added another texture! Can't we get it from the texture atlas? Well, yes, you can!

If you run the texture packing process again, you will see that the font image is now in the texture atlas, which means we can change the code to the following:

```
bitmapFont = new BitmapFont(new BitmapFont.BitmapFontData(Gdx.files.
internal("score.fnt"), false), textureAtlas.findRegion("score"),
true);
```

Awesome! However, we can take it even further. Remember the asset manager we introduced? Remember how it had that brilliant ability to keep track of assets we have loaded? Well, we can use it for our font!

In our `LoadingScreen` class, we can add the following code to the `show()` method:

```
public void show() {
  // Code omitted for brevity
```

```
BitmapFontLoader.BitmapFontParameter bitmapFontParameter =
new BitmapFontLoader.BitmapFontParameter();
bitmapFontParameter.atlasName = "flappee_bee_assets.atlas";
flappeeBeeGame.getAssetManager().load("score.fnt",
BitmapFont.class, bitmapFontParameter);
}
```

In the preceding code, we created a parameter object that we can use to specify where in the texture atlas our font is coming from, among other things. We then tell the asset manager to load our font.

Then, in our `GameScreen` class, we can change our `BitmapFont` creation code to the following:

```
bitmapFont = flappeeBeeGame.getAssetManager().get("score.fnt");
```

Perfect! Our game textures are all in one place and are centrally managed and we have less complex code to boot!

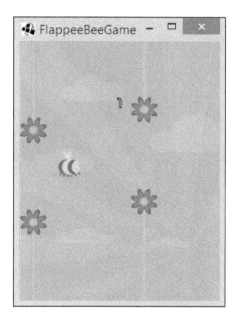

As you can see from the preceding screenshot, here is my font being rendered!

You may be wondering through all this why we didn't touch the **Menu** screen at all. Well, here is your chance to take what you have read in this chapter and apply it yourself!

Summary

In this chapter, we took a step back from creating a game so that you could learn about how LibGDX can help us to make games that are better performing, easier to maintain, and are neater overall. We looked at asset managing and the tools that LibGDX has to help us control and manage our assets throughout the game's life cycle, simplifying the code required to load and dispose of assets. We then looked at how to reduce our game's demand on the hardware it runs on by reducing our textures and transforming them into a single texture asset—a texture atlas. We saw how we can have this as a transparent step in our development so the atlas is always up to date. Then, finally, we looked at using our own fonts and exporting them with the Hiero tool and how we can incorporate these into our game using the texture packer and the asset manager to manage the fonts for us.

Coming up in the next chapter: we will start a new game. The game we will see next will be similar to that of a certain Italian plumber's first outing back in 1985. We will go through how to make a platformer, looking at tile maps to populate the screen and moving a character around with simple physics utilizing a two-stage collision detection system.

6
Onto the Next Platform...Game

In this chapter, we are going to look at making our next game! This is going to be based off a classic game, Super Mario Bros. Yes, that's right! We are going to look at making a platformer, a genre made famous and popularized by the famous plumber and the big N. In this chapter, we will look at reusing everything we have learned to give us a head start, and then we will get introduced to a new tool named Tiled — a tile map editor to help us build a simple level. We will then take the output generated from that tool, and import it into our game using the Tile Map API that LibGDX has. Next, we will add our character and introduce collision detection between our character and the tile map we have. Finally, we will add a simple collectable that our character can collect while traversing our new world.

So, get ready to make our next game! We will cover the following topics in this chapter:

- Why and what is a platformer?
- Reusing what we already have
- Tile maps – introducing tile map editor
- Introducing Pete
- Collision detection revisited
- Adding a collectable

Why and what is a platformer?

Platforming is a classic gaming genre and concept. So, it makes complete sense that we should look at it. Every gamer will have played one at some point, jumping through the levels, collecting power ups, and defeating the foe with the aim of getting to the end.

Before we dive in, I feel we just need to cover what a platformer is, just in case there are people who are unaware.

A platform game usually involves the player character jumping through a game level, essentially going platform to platform, dodging obstacles, and avoiding traps, such as falling off the edge and out of the game. They can range from simplistic affairs to complex efforts where advanced concepts are involved, such as racing against a clock, having the player perform double jumps or wall jumps, or negotiating movable platforms.

Traditionally, a platform game has the player traveling from the left to the right of the screen in a linear fashion. The screen will follow the player in what is known as side-scrolling, allowing the level to be larger than the screen itself.

To start with, our game will be self-contained on the screen. We will look at creating a side-scrolling game in the next chapter.

Introducing Pete the platformer

Our new game is going to star our new character Pete, in what we will call Pete the Platformer.

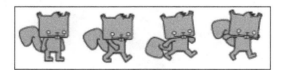

Pete will have full movement from the left to right, as well as jumping.

Game reuse

Right before we dive into looking at tile maps and creating a wonderful world in which Pete will live, we need to set up our project.

Once you have created the project using the LibGDX setup tool — you should be good at that by now — we will need to create a `GameScreen` class as before, extending the `ScreenAdapter` class.

Remember, we will need the following objects in our `GameScreen` class:

- `ShapeRenderer`
- `Viewport`
- `Camera`
- `SpriteBatch`

As this is a platformer, we are going to want a view that is more landscape than we have had before. So, we will have a world size of 640 x 480:

```
private static final float WORLD_WIDTH = 640;
private static final float WORLD_HEIGHT = 480;
```

Then, we will keep the core functionality for updating and rendering. So, hopefully, your `GameScreen` class looks like the following:

```
public class GameScreen extends ScreenAdapter {
  private static final float WORLD_WIDTH = 640;
  private static final float WORLD_HEIGHT = 480;
  private ShapeRenderer shapeRenderer;
  private Viewport viewport;
  private Camera camera;
  private SpriteBatch batch;
  private final PeteGame peteGame;
  public GameScreen(PeteGame peteGame) {
    this.peteGame = peteGame;
  }

  @Override
  public void resize(int width, int height) {
    viewport.update(width, height);
  }

  @Override
  public void show() {
    camera = new OrthographicCamera();
    camera.position.set(WORLD_WIDTH / 2, WORLD_HEIGHT / 2, 0);
    camera.update();
    viewport = new FitViewport(WORLD_WIDTH, WORLD_HEIGHT, camera);
    shapeRenderer = new ShapeRenderer();
    batch = new SpriteBatch();
  }

  @Override
```

```
    public void render(float delta) {
      update(delta);
      clearScreen();
      draw();
      drawDebug();
    }

    private void update(float delta) {
    }

    private void clearScreen() {
      Gdx.gl.glClearColor(Color.BLACK.r, Color.BLACK.g,
      Color.BLACK.b, Color.BLACK.a);
      Gdx.gl.glClear(GL20.GL_COLOR_BUFFER_BIT);
    }

    private void draw() {
      batch.setProjectionMatrix(camera.projection);
      batch.setTransformMatrix(camera.view);
      batch.begin();
      batch.end();
    }

    private void drawDebug() {
      shapeRenderer.setProjectionMatrix(camera.projection);
      shapeRenderer.setTransformMatrix(camera.view);
      shapeRenderer.begin(ShapeRenderer.ShapeType.Line);
      shapeRenderer.end();
    }
  }
```

Hopefully, the preceding code listing shouldn't now come to you as a surprise.

Next, we will need to have a loading screen in place, along with AssetManager that we now know and love.

Let's update our game class with the addition of AssetManager:

```
public class PeteGame extends Game {
  private final AssetManager assetManager = new AssetManager();

  @Override
  public void create() {
    setScreen(new LoadingScreen(this));
  }

  public AssetManager getAssetManager() {
```

```
        return assetManager;
    }
}
```

Hopefully, your IDE at this stage will be complaining that the LoadingScreen class
doesn't exist, which is good, as it doesn't! Let's create it.

Our LoadingScreen class is going to be very similar to what we had before, except
we will remove the Flappee Bee references. So, go ahead, create and update your
LoadingScreen class.

Done? Excellent. Hopefully, it will look like the following code:

```java
public class LoadingScreen extends ScreenAdapter {
    private static final float WORLD_WIDTH = 640;
    private static final float WORLD_HEIGHT = 480;
    private static final float PROGRESS_BAR_WIDTH = 100;
    private static final float PROGRESS_BAR_HEIGHT = 25;
    private ShapeRenderer shapeRenderer;
    private Viewport viewport;
    private OrthographicCamera
    camera;
    private float progress = 0;
    private final PeteGame peteGame;
    public LoadingScreen(PeteGame peteGame) {
        this.peteGame = peteGame;
    }

    @Override
    public void resize(int width, int height) {
        viewport.update(width, height);
    }

    @Override
    public void show() {
        camera = new OrthographicCamera();
        camera.position.set(WORLD_WIDTH / 2, WORLD_HEIGHT / 2, 0);
        camera.update();
        viewport = new FitViewport(WORLD_WIDTH, WORLD_HEIGHT, camera);
        shapeRenderer = new ShapeRenderer();
    }

    @Override
    public void render(float delta) {
        update();
```

```
    clearScreen();
    draw();
  }

  @Override
  public void dispose() {
    shapeRenderer.dispose();
  }

  private void update() {
    if (peteGame.getAssetManager().update()) {
      peteGame.setScreen(new GameScreen(peteGame));
    } else {
      progress = peteGame.getAssetManager().getProgress();
    }
  }

  private void clearScreen() {
    Gdx.gl.glClearColor(Color.BLACK.r, Color.BLACK.g,
    Color.BLACK.b, Color.BLACK.a);
    Gdx.gl.glClear(GL20.GL_COLOR_BUFFER_BIT);
  }

  private void draw() {
    shapeRenderer.setProjectionMatrix(camera.projection);
    shapeRenderer.setTransformMatrix(camera.view);
    shapeRenderer.begin(ShapeRenderer.ShapeType.Filled);
    shapeRenderer.setColor(Color.WHITE);
    shapeRenderer.rect(
      (WORLD_WIDTH - PROGRESS_BAR_WIDTH) / 2, WORLD_HEIGHT / 2 -
      PROGRESS_BAR_HEIGHT / 2,
      progress * PROGRESS_BAR_WIDTH, PROGRESS_BAR_HEIGHT);
    shapeRenderer.end();
  }
}
```

We have a nice little platform (pun intended!) to start building our game. If you run our project, you should get a nice 640x480px black square on your screen.

If so, we are good to go! If not, just revisit the previous chapters and the games we made, to see if you missed something.

Tile maps – mapping all over the world!

When platformers first started appearing, on the early game consoles, they took a tile approach to their levels. Levels were split up into cells, and then each cell would be assigned an ID that would correspond to a tile in perhaps a texture atlas—ooh, we know about them! This had the great benefit of reducing the memory footprint, because you could build an entire level from just a handful of tiles, and that is exactly what we are going to do.

Introducing Tiled

When we build our level out of tiles, we are going to need a tool to help us visualize the level as we go ahead. You could go and do it all by hand, drawing it on paper, noting IDs and cells, and then updating a text file somewhere; however, that will be slow and cumbersome—take it from someone who used to do that!

So what can we use? Well, I have always been fond of a free-to-use tool called Tiled (for more information, visit `http://www.mapeditor.org/`). It has an amazing feature set, multiple layers, and stamping collections of tiles to help with larger levels. We won't be using all these features. The aim here is to get you used to using a tool like this, and then you can spread your wings and dive deep into what it can do when it comes to your own game!

Once you have downloaded Tiled, open it up and we will begin!

Creating a new map

Go to the **File** drop-down menu and select **New** as an option. You will then be presented with a **New Map** dialog, such as follows:

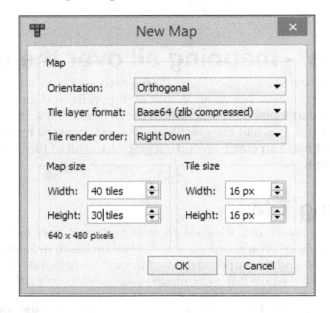

The first section talks about how our map is going to be saved and presented. We can keep the same settings as shown in the preceding screenshot. We want our orientation as **Orthogonal** as we are working on a 2D game. The format, while at this stage, isn't really that important, but having the map saved in a compressed format is fine. Finally, in this section, we need the render order to be **Right Down**, as this is how LibGDX will handle reading and rendering the map.

The next two sections cover the map properties. Our art work is 16x16px tiles and our world is 640x480, so we can set it up with the preceding settings.

Finally, save the project. I have called mine `pete.tmx` and I have saved it into our assets directory in our core project.

Hopefully, your screen should look like mine.

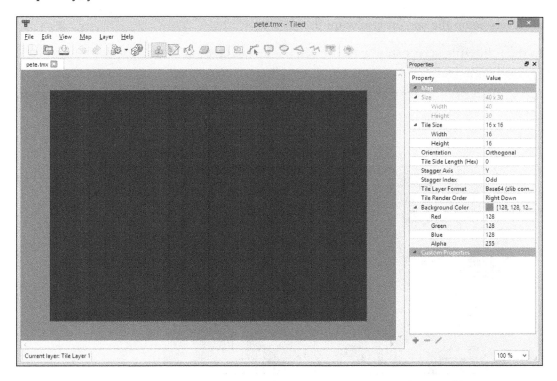

Our next step is to add our tile texture atlas to the tile layer, so that we can start creating a level.

To do this, we need to go to the **Map** file option and select the **New Tileset** menu option. From here, we can import our texture atlas that represents our tile set.

Our texture we are using is called `floor.png` and here is how it looks.

Essentially, we have 18 tiles at a size of 16x16 pixels.

If the tilesets windows don't appear after you import the asset, you can enable it by going to the **View** option, clicking on the **Views and ToolBars** option, and then selecting **tilesets**.

Finally, we can build our level. If you have a play around with Tiled, you will find it is quite straightforward to create a level. You select the tile you wish to use and then click where on the screen you want it.

In the following screenshot, you can see the level I created. Going forward, I will be using this in the game.

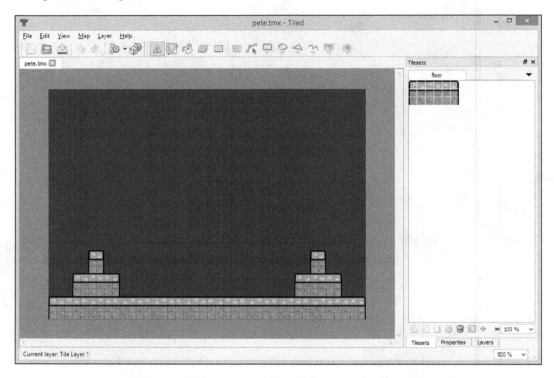

Just save the tile map and we are ready.

Great! Now that we have our level, we just need to load it into LibGDX!

The LibGDX Tile Map API

Now that we have our lovely TMX file created by Tiled, we need to load it in LibGDX so that we can render it. We are going to do this using our AssetManager object, as it will do the heavy lifting for us. However, it doesn't support the TMX file out of the box, so we need to tell it how to load the TMX file.

To tell the `AssetManager` object how to load the TMX file, we assign a loader to class type. In this case, our class we want to have once loaded is `TiledMap` and the loader is the `TmxMapLoader` class. For those interested, visit the wiki page for Tile Maps in LibGDX, at `https://github.com/libgdx/libgdx/wiki/Tile-maps`.

Adding the loader is straightforward in the `create()` method of our `PeteGame` class. Update it so it looks like the following code:

```
public void create() {
    assetManager.setLoader(TiledMap.class, new TmxMapLoader(new
    InternalFileHandleResolver()));
    setScreen(new LoadingScreen(this));
}
```

Here we are just instructing the asset manager that if we want to load an object of type `TiledMap`, then use the `TmxMapLoader` class.

Next, we need to update our `LoadingScreen` class to load the tile map. Update the `show()` method as follows:

```
public void show() {
    //Code omitted for brevity
    peteGame.getAssetManager().load("pete.tmx", TiledMap.class);
}
```

The final step to loading our map is to grab it from the asset manager, so that it is ready to render. To do this, we need to create a reference to the `TiledMap` class in the `GameScreen` class as follows:

```
private TiledMap tiledMap;
```

Then, in our `show()` method, let's call the `AssetManager` object to get our object:

```
public void show() {
    //Code omitted for brevity
    tiledMap = peteGame.getAssetManager().get("pete.tmx");
}
```

Excellent. If you run the project now, you will still find we will have a blank screen; this is because we are not rendering the map yet! To do this, we need to use the `OrthogonalTiledMapRenderer` class.

So, in our `GameScreen` class, let's add our `OrthogonalTiledMapRenderer` class:

```
private OrthogonalTiledMapRenderer orthogonalTiledMapRenderer;
public void show() {
    camera = new OrthographicCamera();
    viewport = new FitViewport(WORLD_WIDTH, WORLD_HEIGHT, camera);
```

```
        viewport.apply(true);
        shapeRenderer = new ShapeRenderer();
        batch = new SpriteBatch();
        tiledMap = peteGame.getAssetManager().get("pete.tmx");
        orthogonalTiledMapRenderer = new
        OrthogonalTiledMapRenderer(tiledMap, batch);
        orthogonalTiledMapRenderer.setView(camera);
    }
```

So in the preceding code, we have added our renderer. We then construct it with the tile map that we loaded, and we pass in the `SpriteBatch` instance. Finally, we set up the view by passing in the camera. We have also changed how our camera is centered, by calling `apply(true)` on our viewport.

Finally, we just call the `render()` method in our `draw()` method as follows:

```
    private void draw() {
        batch.setProjectionMatrix(camera.projection);
        batch.setTransformMatrix(camera.view);
        orthogonalTiledMapRenderer.render();
    }
```

As you type out the preceding code, you will find that the renderer has a few different options for rendering the map. By default, we are telling it to render all the layers that exist in the map, currently one. However, when you start to do more complex maps, you might have many layers, and you might wish to render only certain layers or render them in specific order. You may, hopefully, have also noticed that we don't call `begin()` or `end()` on the `SpriteBatch` object. This is because it is done for us in the tile map renderer object! Pretty neat hey?

Excellent. If you run the project, you should get the level that you created appearing on the screen.

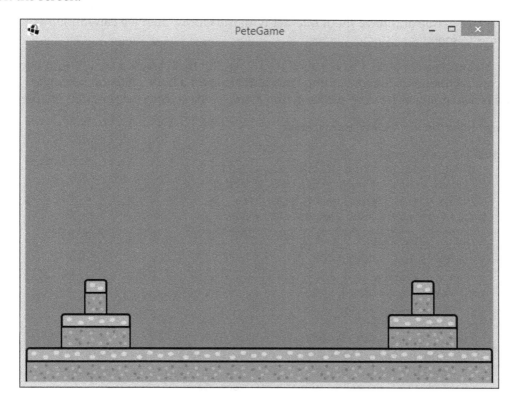

Introducing Pete

So far we have created a level using Tiled, and we have implemented tile maps in LibGDX so that we can see that level. The next step is to introduce our characters into this world and have them interact with the surroundings.

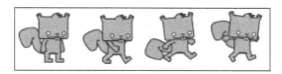

The preceding image shows Pete, our lovely squirrel! He has four different poses, two for walking and one each for jumping up and down.

Adding our character

Before we add our textures to Pete, let's go through the process of creating our character in code and have them interact with the world, then we can implement the animations.

Let's create class for Pete, I have called it `Pete` and in that class we are going create the core components for controlling Pete, and also add a basic collision rectangle. This class is also going to be very similar to the `Flappee` class from the previous chapters.

Here is how the `Pete` class should look:

```
public class Pete {
  private static final float MAX_X_SPEED = 2;
  private static final float MAX_Y_SPEED = 2;
  public static final int WIDTH = 16;
  public static final int HEIGHT = 15;
  private final Rectangle collisionRectangle = new Rectangle(C, 0,
  WIDTH, HEIGHT);
  private float x = 0;
  private float y = 0;
  private float xSpeed = 0;
  private float ySpeed = 0;
  public void update() {
    Input input = Gdx.input;
    if (input.isKeyPressed(Input.Keys.RIGHT)) {
      xSpeed = MAX_X_SPEED;
    } else if (input.isKeyPressed(Input.Keys.LEFT)) {
      xSpeed = -MAX_X_SPEED;
    } else {
      xSpeed = 0;
    }
    x += xSpeed;
    y += ySpeed;
    updateCollisionRectangle();
  }
  public void drawDebug(ShapeRenderer shapeRenderer) {
    shapeRenderer.rect(collisionRectangle.x, collisionRectangle.y,
    collisionRectangle.width, collisionRectangle.height);
  }

  private void updateCollisionRectangle() {
    collisionRectangle.setPosition(x, y);
  }
}
```

In the preceding code, we first start off by setting up some parameters for Pete, such as maximum speed and how big in world units Pete will be, and we will also define a `Rectangle` object that we will use for collision purposes. Finally, we define variables that hold information about where in the world Pete is, and his current speed.

Next, we define an `update()` method. This will be called on every game loop cycle we poll for the player input, depending on the input we assigned for the speed at which Pete should be moving. So, in this case, let's show that code snippet again:

```
if (input.isKeyPressed(Input.Keys.RIGHT)) {
  xSpeed = MAX_X_SPEED;
} else if (input.isKeyPressed(Input.Keys.LEFT)) {
  xSpeed = -MAX_X_SPEED;
} else {
  xSpeed = 0;
}
```

If the player is pressing right, then we will set the speed to be the maximum speed. This means Pete will move right—remember our 0,0 position is in the bottom left— then, if left is pressed, we set the speed to be the negative of the maximum speed, which means that when we apply it to our x and y variables, it will move Pete left. Finally, if neither is pressed, then we set the speed to 0.

The final part of the update method is to apply our speed to our x and y variables, and then update our collision rectangle to the new position—similar to how we did it in our Flappee Bee game.

The final step to introducing Pete into the game is to add the `Pete` class to the `GameScreen` class.

First, add a reference:

```
private Pete pete;
```

Then, update our `show()` method to instantiate our class.

```
public void show() {
  // Code omitted for brevity
  pete = new Pete();
}
```

Finally, call the `update()` method in the `GameScreen` class' `update()` method, and the `drawDebug()` method in the corresponding `drawDebug()` method:

```
private void update(float delta) {
  pete.update();
}

private void drawDebug() {
  shapeRenderer.setProjectionMatrix(camera.projection);
  shapeRenderer.setTransformMatrix(camera.view);
  shapeRenderer.begin(ShapeRenderer.ShapeType.Line);
  pete.drawDebug(shapeRenderer);
  shapeRenderer.end();
}
```

Superb! Now if you run the project, you should get a white box appearing in the bottom-left corner of your screen that you can control with the left and right arrows keys on your keyboard!

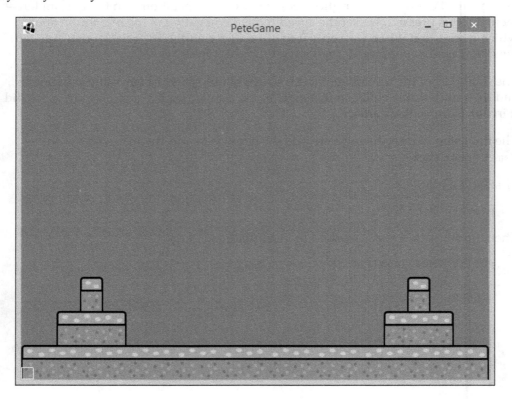

Making Pete jump!

You may have noticed a couple of things.

- Pete is probably over the top of the level you made—we will come to this.
- Pete can only move left and right, and can disappear off the edge of your screen.

Before we address the first point, let's address the second point. As we discussed at the start of this chapter, a platformer involves making the character jump from platform to platform. Well, Pete can't jump! Let's make Pete jump!

Let's consider what we need to do to achieve a platforming style jumping mechanism, as, unfortunately, it isn't as simple as it was moving Pete left or right. There are certain rules we want to obey.

- We want to jump to a maximum height, no indefinite jumping.
- We don't want to let the player jump until Pete has landed, otherwise we inadvertently give them a flying capability.
- We don't want to block the player moving left or right during the jump.

Hopefully, those rules sound quite reasonable for a platformer. Now, we know what we would like to achieve, so let's start by stopping Pete from leaving the screen.

First, we need to provide a way for the game to update Pete's position for when it is decided that he has left the screen. In our `Pete` class, let's add the following methods:

```
public void setPosition(float x, float y) {
  this.x = x;
  this.y = y;
  updateCollisionRectangle();
}

public float getX() {
  return x;
}

public float getY() {
  return y;
}
```

Here we have added the ability to query the x and y position of Pete, while being able to set the position which then updates the collision rectangle.

Next, in our `GameScreen` class, we need to interrogate Pete to find out his position and then put him back into view if needed. So, go back to our `GameScreen` class and add the following method:

```
private void stopPeteLeavingTheScreen() {
  if (pete.getY() < 0) {
    pete.setPosition(pete.getX(), 0);
  }
  if (pete.getX() < 0) {
    pete.setPosition(0, pete.getY());
  }
  if (pete.getX() + Pete.WIDTH > WORLD_WIDTH) {
    pete.setPosition(WORLD_WIDTH - Pete.WIDTH,
    pete.getY());
  }
}
```

Hopefully, this code is straightforward to read. We are essentially checking if Pete has left via the bottom of the screen, then the left, and then the right. You might be wondering why on the final `if` statement we are looking at Pete's width. Well, if we don't do that, then he will leave the screen before our code to reposition him is called, as, remember, our coordinates all work off of the bottom-left side.

Finally, add a call to `pete` method in our `update()` method:

```
private void update(float delta) {
  pete.update();
  stopPeteLeavingTheScreen();
}
```

Brilliant! Now when you run the game, Pete should not be able to leave the screen.

Ok, so now that we have sorted it out, we can start thinking about making Pete jump. So, to conform to our rules, we need to have two variables that will help us control Pete's jumping ability:

```
private boolean blockJump = false;
private float jumpYDistance = 0;
```

Add the preceding two variables to our `Pete` class. The `blockJump` variable will be used to signal to not allow any more up movement and `jumpYDistance` will be used to keep track of how far Pete will have traveled on the y plane while jumping up. Next, we should define what is the maximum distance (or height) we want Pete to be able to jump:

```
private static final float MAX_JUMP_DISTANCE = 3 * HEIGHT;
```

Add the preceding line to `Pete`; here we are using a value of three times the height of Pete. This may or may not fit the game. The beauty of making games is we can always change these values to help decide what feels fun and enjoyable.

Now that we have those in place, we can start adding some logic to triggering the jump. Since we are using the arrow keys to control Pete, let's use the up arrow to trigger the jump action. In the `update()` method of our `Pete` class, let's insert the following code:

```
if (input.isKeyPressed(Input.Keys.UP) && !blockJump) {
  ySpeed = MAX_Y_SPEED;
  jumpYDistance += ySpeed;
  blockJump = jumpYDistance > MAX_JUMP_DISTANCE;
} else {
  ySpeed = -MAX_Y_SPEED;
  blockJump = jumpYDistance > 0;
}
```

Place it just before the following lines of code:

```
x += xSpeed;
y += ySpeed;
```

"What are we telling Pete to do here?" You might be thinking; well, I am going to tell you. So, if the player presses up and our `blockJump` variable is `false`, we will set the `ySpeed` variable to the maximum value, we will then increment our variable, `jumpYDistance`, to keep track of how far Pete has moved, and then we will decide to block the jump action if that distance traveled has gone above our maximum we declared before.

If the player isn't pressing up, we set the y value to be the negative maximum and we will block the jump if the distance traveled is above zero. The reason for doing this is if the player has released the up key before Pete has traveled the full distance of his jump. This will allow the player to make smaller jumps.

With that added, if you run the project now and press up, Pete will jump. Now, press up again. Oh, Pete didn't jump. Well, we should have expected that as we haven't reset our jump blocking variable. That won't make a good game if Pete can only jump once.

So, what we should do is provide way for the game to tell Pete if he has landed on something. Now, we haven't implemented our collision detection on our tile map yet, but we do land before Pete goes off the bottom of the screen.

Let's add a `landed()` method to our `Pete` class:

```
public void landed() {
  blockJump = false;
  jumpYDistance = 0;
  ySpeed = 0;
}
```

As you can see in the preceding code, we are just resetting our jump control parameters. All we have to do now is have this called from our `GameScreen` class. So, we just need to update our `stopPeteLeavingTheScreen()` method as follows:

```
private void stopPeteLeavingTheScreen() {
  if (pete.getY() < 0) {
    pete.setPosition(pete.getX(), 0);
    pete.landed();
  }
  if (pete.getX() < 0) {
    pete.setPosition(0, pete.getY());
  }
  if (pete.getX() + Pete.WIDTH > WORLD_WIDTH) {
    pete.setPosition(WORLD_WIDTH - Pete.WIDTH, pete.getY());
  }
}
```

Here we have just added the call when Pete has been deemed to leave the screen from the bottom.

If you run the project now, you will find that you make Pete, or the square that represents Pete, jump and bounce all over the place!

So there is the basics, of getting a jump mechanic going. Obviously, games will take this far further when refining the controls. For example, you would have acceleration and deceleration factors to consider, which would make the jumping feel a touch more realistic, for example, Pete could gradually slow down as he reached the top of his jump capability. Also, the concept of gravity could be introduced, which would affect the movement. But for what we are looking to achieve here, this will do!

Adding our artwork

With Pete jumping about and moving around, albeit in square form, we can now look to bring him alive by added the Pete texture.

Our first step is to add the texture to our asset manager; we can do this in the `LoadingScreen` class. Let's update the `show()` method with the following line of code:

```
peteGame.getAssetManager().load("pete.png", Texture.class);
```

Next, we need to update our `Pete` class to take this texture and turn it into an animation and individual `TextureRegion` objects. So, in our `Pete` class, let's add the following code:

```
private float animationTimer = 0;
private final Animation walking;
private final TextureRegion standing;
private final TextureRegion jumpUp;
private final TextureRegion jumpDown;
public Pete(Texture texture) {
  TextureRegion[] regions = TextureRegion.split(texture, WIDTH,
  HEIGHT)[0];
  walking = new Animation(0.25F, regions[0], regions[1]);
  walking.setPlayMode(Animation.PlayMode.LOOP);
  standing = regions[0];
  jumpUp = regions[2];
  jumpDown = regions[3];
}
```

From the preceding code, you can see we have added references to the textures and to the animation object we are going to set up. Next we have our constructor, here we are passing in the texture that represents Pete and we split it into the tiles. We create our animation; this should all feel familiar as we did essentially the same thing with Flappee Bee in the previous chapter.

Next, we need to update our `update()` method so that we can update our animation timer:

```
public void update(float delta) {
  animationTimer += delta;
  //Code omitted for brevity
}
```

Finally, we need to add a `draw()` method. Here, we will pass in our `SpriteBatch` object, considering which image of Pete to draw, depending on what he is doing:

```
public void draw(Batch batch) {
  TextureRegion toDraw = standing;
  if (xSpeed != 0) {
    toDraw = walking.getKeyFrame(animationTimer);
  }
  if (ySpeed > 0) {
    toDraw = jumpUp;
  } else if (ySpeed < 0) {
    toDraw = jumpDown;
  }

  if (xSpeed < 0) {
    if (!toDraw.isFlipX()) toDraw.flip(true,false);
  } else if (xSpeed > 0) {
    if (toDraw.isFlipX()) toDraw.flip(true,false);
  }

  batch.draw(toDraw, x, y);
}
```

So, in the preceding code, we start off assuming Pete is standing. Then, depending on the speed at which he is moving, we assigned either a frame from the walk animation or the jumping textures. The reason we have the jump textures check last is that even if there is a non-zero value for `xSpeed`, we still want the jump texture.

Finally, in this method, we look to flip the texture if Pete is facing the other way.

With that added, update your GameScreen class to reflect our changes to the Pete class. I trust you can do this! Once you have, run the project, and we should get the following output:

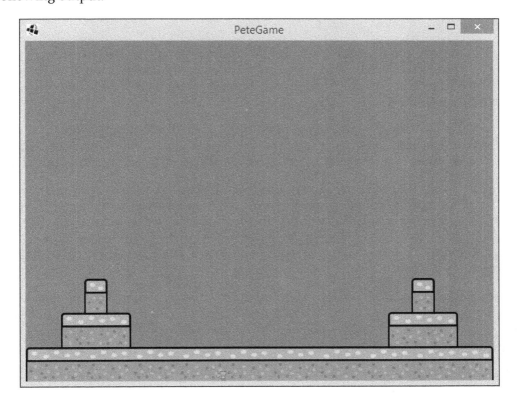

As you can see from the preceding screenshot, and hopefully your screen too, Pete is being fully animated!

Now onto the collision detection.

Collision detection

So here we are. We have Pete wandering around on the screen, with the ability to jump, and looking pretty snazzy. We need to take the next step and have him interact with the level we created.

When it comes to collision detection, there is a vast array of different methods, concepts, and techniques that get used when making platformers. However, for what we are trying to achieve here, giving you a taster on using LibGDX to make games, we can take a simplistic approach.

The approach we are going to take is a two-phase detection. Firstly, we find out what cells Pete is currently covering, and then we work out if these cells contain the solid ground tiles. Then, we will resolve the collision by moving Pete out of the cells area.

So, to start with, we need to work out which cells Pete currently covers. We can do this by, firstly, using Pete's position and size, and then converting that to cells. We know that our level is 640x480 units big and our cells are 16x16 and, therefore, know that our grid is 40x30 cells. Given that we know Pete is of size 16x16 as well, we know, therefore, that the maximum amount of cells he could cover is four, with the minimum being one.

So let's start coding! First, we should define a class that will contain the information about the cell that we need. This will know the cell and the x and y cell coordinates that we will require. I created an inner class in `GameScreen` called `CollisionCell`. The following is the code:

```
private class CollisionCell {
    private final TiledMapTileLayer.Cell cell;
    private final int cellX;
    private final int cellY;

    public CollisionCell(TiledMapTileLayer.Cell cell, int cellX, int
    cellY) {
        this.cell = cell;
        this.cellX = cellX;
        this.cellY = cellY;
    }

    public boolean isEmpty() {
        return cell == null;
    }
}
```

As you can see in the preceding code, it simply holds information. The only addition is that we add an isEmpty() method, as if the cell is null, and it is a blank cell.

In our GameScreen class, let's now create a method called whichCellsDoesPeteCover(). This is essentially going to figure out which cells Pete covers. In this method, we will look at Pete's x and y position in the level, and then query the tile map for the cells that he covers. The following code shows how this is achieved:

```
private Array<CollisionCell> whichCellsDoesPeteCover() {
   float x = pete.getX();
   float y = pete.getY();
   Array<CollisionCell> cellsCovered = new Array<CollisionCell>();
   float cellX = x / CELL_SIZE;
   float cellY = y / CELL_SIZE;

   int bottomLeftCellX = MathUtils.floor(cellX);
   int bottomLeftCellY = MathUtils.floor(cellY);

   TiledMapTileLayer tiledMapTileLayer = (TiledMapTileLayer)
   tiledMap.getLayers().get(0);

   cellsCovered.add(new
   CollisionCell(tiledMapTileLayer.getCell(bottomLeftCellX,
   bottomLeftCellY), bottomLeftCellX, bottomLeftCellY));

   if (cellX % 1 != 0 && cellY % 1 != 0) {
      int topRightCellX = bottomLeftCellX + 1;
      int topRightCellY = bottomLeftCellY + 1;
      cellsCovered.add(new
      CollisionCell(tiledMapTileLayer.getCell(topRightCellX,
      topRightCellY), topRightCellX, topRightCellY));
   }

   if (cellX % 1 != 0) {
      int bottomRightCellX = bottomLeftCellX + 1;
      int bottomRightCellY = bottomLeftCellY;
      cellsCovered.add(new
      CollisionCell(tiledMapTileLayer.getCell(bottomRightCellX,
      bottomRightCellY), bottomRightCellX, bottomRightCellY));
   }

   if (cellY % 1 != 0) {
      int topLeftCellX = bottomLeftCellX;
      int topLeftCellY = bottomLeftCellY + 1;
```

```
    cellsCovered.add(new
    CollisionCell(tiledMapTileLayer.getCell(topLeftCellX,
    topLeftCellY), topLeftCellX, topLeftCellY));
  }
  return cellsCovered;
}
```

In the preceding code, we first get Pete's x and y position; we then divide that by the size of a cell, which is currently 16 units. This gives us a decimal value of the cell x and y in the grid.

We gain access to `TiledMapTiledLayer` by cheekily accessing the zero element of the layers array of the `TiledMap`. We can get away with this because we only have one layer. As your games get more and more complex, there will be multiple layers; here is where you can start naming the layers and requesting them by name.

Next, we floor those values to give us the bottom-left cell that Pete covers. There is a chance that this cell is the only cell Pete covers; however, more often than not, there will be more than one. That is where the next few lines of code come in; we take the modulus of the `cellX` and `cellY` values to give us the remainder. We can use this to determine if Pete overlays another cell. So, for example, if the `cellX` value is 3.25, then the modulus will be 0.25, and, therefore, we know that the next cell along will contain Pete. We repeat this for the y coordinate, and then if both have a remainder, we grab the top right most cell.

Finally, we return those cells. This is a good start that we know the cells. Next we need to look at them and decide how to make Pete react. Luckily, the way `TiledMapLayer` works is that if there isn't a tile in the map, then it will be null!

So, our next step is to filter out the array of the null values. Let's add the following method:

```
private Array<CollisionCell> filterOutNonTiledCells(Array<CollisionCe
ll> cells) {
  for (Iterator<CollisionCell> iter = cells.iterator();
  iter.hasNext(); ) {
    CollisionCell collisionCell = iter.next();
    if (collisionCell.isEmpty()) {
      iter.remove();
    }
  }
  return cells;
}
```

Here we are simply iterating over the array and ditching the null value. This means that when Pete is in open space, our array will be empty!

Now I think we are ready to handle a collision between Pete and the level!

The first part we will look at is handling Pete landing on the level. If I were you, I would add a line of code to set a starting position for Pete, so that he is out in the open and can fall on to the level. Use the setPosition() method to achieve this; it might take some trial and error, but have a play around. Initially, he should just fall to the bottom of the screen.

Next, let's start to hook up the code we have written. Create a method in GameScreen called handlePeteCollision(), and let's populate it with the following code:

```
private void handlePeteCollision() {
  Array<CollisionCell> peteCells = whichCellsDoesPeteCover();
  peteCells = filterOutNonTiledCells(peteCells);
  for (CollisionCell cell : peteCells) {
    float cellLevelX = cell.cellX * CELL_SIZE;
    float cellLevelY = cell.cellY * CELL_SIZE;
    Rectangle intersection = new Rectangle();
    Intersector.intersectRectangles(pete.getCollisionRectangle(),
    new Rectangle(cellLevelX, cellLevelY, CELL_SIZE, CELL_SIZE),
    intersection);
    if (intersection.getHeight() < intersection.getWidth()) {
      pete.setPosition(pete.getX(), intersection.getY() +
      intersection.getHeight());
      pete.landed();
    } else if (intersection.getWidth() < intersection.getHeight())
    {
      if (intersection.getX() == pete.getX()) {
        pete.setPosition(intersection.getX() +
        intersection.getWidth(), pete.getY());
      }
      if (intersection.getX() > pete.getX()) {
        pete.setPosition(intersection.getX() - Pete.WIDTH,
        pete.getY());
      }
    }
  }
}
```

Here we call the `whichCellsDoesPeteCover()` method this provides us with cells Pete overlaps, we then filter these, so only cells which are part of the level are left. We are then iterating over these cells, and here we are using a new-to-us class `Intersector`; this class is amazing, it contains an insane amount of helper methods for working out if shapes overlap, and if they do, what the area is that they over lap by. This is really helpful for us as it will do all the heavy work for us.

So how are we using it? Well, we are using the `intersectRectangles()` methods that takes two rectangles that will be checked for overlapping, and then a third that is the area of the overlap. Our two rectangles are Pete's collision zone and the cell that we are currently iterating over, and we then create a third one. Next comes the interesting part, Once we have the overlap, we look to see which is bigger: the height or the width of the overlap. This is important because if we don't take that into consideration, we might end up moving Pete into a position that doesn't make sense in the game. So, we look at if the height of the overlap is less than the width, and if that is the case, then that means Pete is closer to the top or bottom of the cell than the left and right. This means you can move Pete up, the caveat here is that this only deals with Pete falling onto cells, rather than jumping up into those cells. If it is the case that the width is less than the height, we then work out if Pete is to the left or the right of the cell in question, and then move him back accordingly.

Finally, we just need to add a call to the `handlePeteCollision()` method to our `update()` method:

```
private void update(float delta) {
  pete.update(delta);
  stopPeteLeavingTheScreen();
  handlePeteCollision();
}
```

Hopefully, now when you run the project, you will have Pete jumping around your level.

Excellent! We have the beginnings of a platformer; while it won't rival Super Mario at this point, hopefully, it gives you a great starting point for your future platforming games.

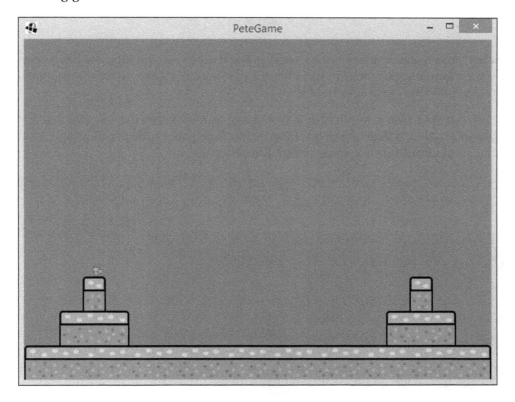

Adding a collectable

We almost have a platforming game! Admittedly, it doesn't do much—yet! But hey, let's change that. One of the main components of a platformer is having something for the player to collect. Considering Pete is a squirrel, I guess it is only right that he collects acorns.

To add our collectable to the game, we are going to need to do a couple of things. Firstly, we need to find a way for us to place the collectables in the game in an easy-to-do manner , next, have them successfully load that information into LibGDX, and then, finally, have the interaction between Pete and the acorn.

Our acorn will look as follows:

So, what can we use to place the acorn(s) in the level? Well, luckily, we have been using a certain mapping tool in this chapter that we can use to do this. Yup, that's right! Tiled has the capability to help us.

In Tiled, our first task is to add our acorn image as a tileset so that we can use it. Simply select **New Tileset** from the **Map** menu, navigate to the acorn image, and select it. This should now appear in our **Tilesets** pane.

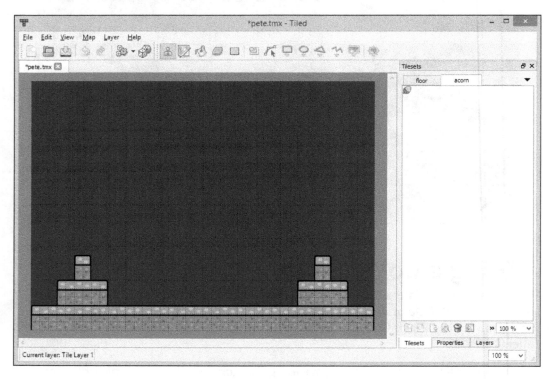

Next, we add a new layer, but this time we are going to add an object layer. From the **Layer** drop-down menu, select **Add Object Layer**. You will now be given the option to name it, call it Collectables.

Make sure the **Collectables** layer is selected, and return to the acorn tileset. Then, select the insert tile button on the toolbar before finally selecting the acorn. Now we can start placing them on the level.

Hopefully, you should end up something like the following screenshot:

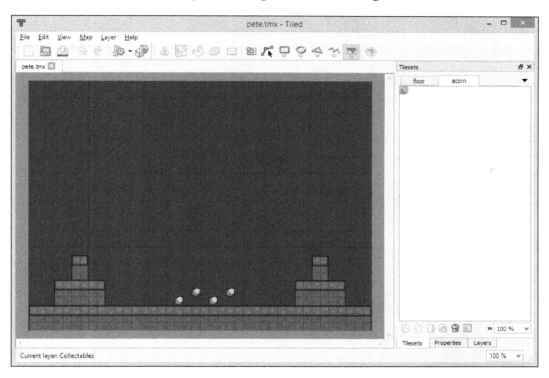

With our acorns placed, our next step is to query the layer in LibGDX to access the location of the acorns.

Our first task here is to create an `Acorn` class, which will contain the texture and location of the acorn. Create the following class:

```
public class Acorn {
  public static final int WIDTH = 16;
  public static final int HEIGHT = 16;
  private final Rectangle collision;
  private final Texture texture;
  private final float x;
  private final float y;
  public Acorn(Texture texture, float x, float y) {
    this.texture = texture;
```

```
    this.x = x;
    this.y = y;
    this.collision = new Rectangle(x,y, WIDTH,HEIGHT);
  }

  public void draw(Batch batch) {
    batch.draw(texture, x, y);
  }
}
```

Let's now add an array of acorns to our GameScreen class:

```
private Array<Acorn> acorns = new Array<Acorn>();
```

Next, we need to add a method to our GameScreen class that will extract the information from the TiledMap object. Again, add the following method to your GameScreen class:

```
private void populateAcorns() {
  MapLayer mapLayer = tiledMap.getLayers().get("Collectables");
  for (MapObject mapObject : mapLayer.getObjects()) {
    acorns.add(
      new Acorn(peteGame.getAssetManager().get("acorn.png",
      Texture.class),
        mapObject.getProperties().get("x", Float.class),
        mapObject.getProperties().get("y", Float.class)
      )
    );
  }
}
```

Here we are requesting the layer from the TiledMap object that we created and called Collectables. Next we are iterating over the MapObject instances that this layer contains. For each MapObject we are creating an Acorn instance and adding to our acorns array. The *x* and *y* coordinates are located in the properties of the MapObject class, hence why we need to extract them like we do. This is actually a pretty neat way, as in the future you could add your own properties in Tiled and then access them this way.

Next, we update our draw() method to render our acorns:

```
private void draw() {
  //Code omitted for brevity
  for (Acorn acorn : acorns) {
    acorn.draw(batch);
  }
```

```
      pete.draw(batch);
      batch.end();
   }
```

Next, we need to add our `populateAcorns()` method call to our `show()` method as follows:

```
public void show() {
   // Code ommitted for brevity
   populateAcorns();
}
```

Finally, we need to add our acorn texture to our asset manager in the loading screen; otherwise, it won't get loaded! So, update the `show()` method of our `LoadingScreen` class with the following code:

```
peteGame.getAssetManager().load("acorn.png", Texture.class);
```

We should now be ready to rock and roll! If you load up the game, you should now be presented with acorns.

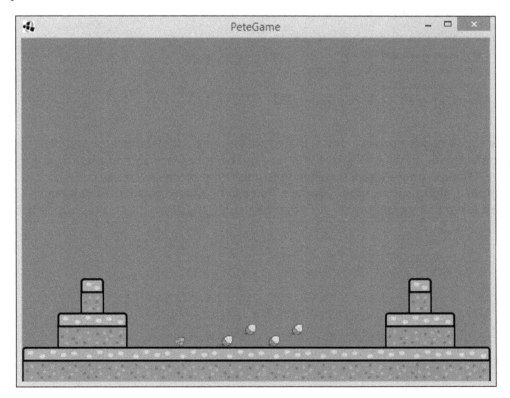

Excellent! We are almost there. You may notice that nothing happens when Pete passes over the acorns. Well, that's what we are going to look at next. Just a quick collision check, then we can remove them from the screen!

Let's add the following code to our `GameScreen` class:

```
private void handlePeteCollisionWithAcorn() {
  for (Iterator<Acorn> iter = acorns.iterator(); iter.hasNext(); )
  {
    Acorn acorn = iter.next();
    if (pete.getCollisionRectangle().
    overlaps(acorn.getCollisionRectangle())){
      iter.remove();
    }
  }
}
```

Here we are iterating over our `Acorn` objects, and checking to see if Pete overlaps with any of them. If they do, we remove the acorn.

Finally, add a call to this method in our `update()` method:

```
private void update(float delta) {
  pete.update(delta);
  stopPeteLeavingTheScreen();
  handlePeteCollision();
  handlePeteCollisionWithAcorn();
}
```

Now if you run the project, you will find that acorns will disappear when Pete comes in contact with them! Awesome! We have the basis here for a good platforming game. While nothing happens when you collect the acorns, we have covered a couple of things in previous chapters that can be reused to have an outcome. I shall leave that as an exercise for you, the reader, to have a go at. You can do it!

Summary

Well, what a chapter we had there. We created the beginnings of our own platforming game, we looked at a really useful tool for level creation, Tiled, and we saw how using LibGDX, we can take the output of Tiled and easily gain access to that information inside our game, using the Tiled Map API. We did some simple collision detection between our characters and the landscape to create our platforming experiencing and then we went through the process of adding game objects — the acorn! — to the game.

Coming up in the next chapter, you will look at taking the game further by having the level bigger than the screen, and introduce scrolling! So, we can really give the game the feel of a platformer. You will also take a look at using sounds in our game so we can bring it to life!

Extending the Platform

7

In the previous chapter, we looked at how to create a simple platform game, where we used a new tool, **Tiled**, that allowed us to create a level and used the Tiled Maps API of LibGDX to bring it to life. However, our game was confined to a single screen. As most of you will be aware, to really take our game to the next level, the level itself should usually be bigger than the screen.

In this chapter, we are going to look at how to extend the level and how to move the camera with Pete as he traverses through our new world. Once we have that, we can then move on to the next topic, which is adding sounds. In this, we will introduce you to the use of music and sound effects. We will cover the following topics in this chapter:

- Increasing the level length
- Introducing camera scroll
- Making sounds
- Playing music

Increasing the level

The idea we have here is simple enough to start off with. I am sure many of you will have figured out that the first thing we need to do is extend the map in Tiled and add some extra tiles to the layer. If so, you would be correct! So, let's reopen Tiled and extend that map.

Just in case you have forgotten, this is where we left our map the last time:

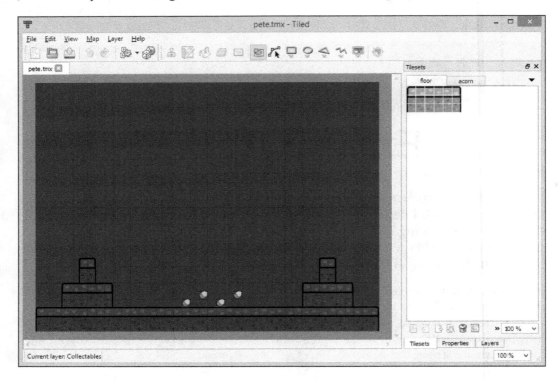

Resizing the Map

If you go to the **Map** drop-down menu and select **Resize Map**, you will be presented with a dialog box that has the current width and height, in tiles, of our map. If you simply double the width value and click on **OK**, you will find that your map is now twice the size of the width, as shown in the following screenshot:

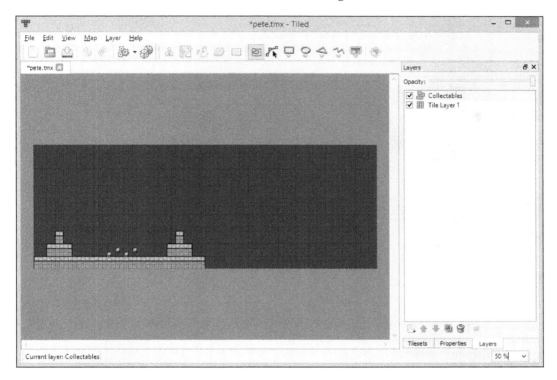

Hopefully, your screen looks somewhat similar to mine. Next, we need to add some more tiles to our **Tile Layer**. Feel free to create yours as you wish; the **Tile Layer** that I created looks like the one shown in the following screenshot:

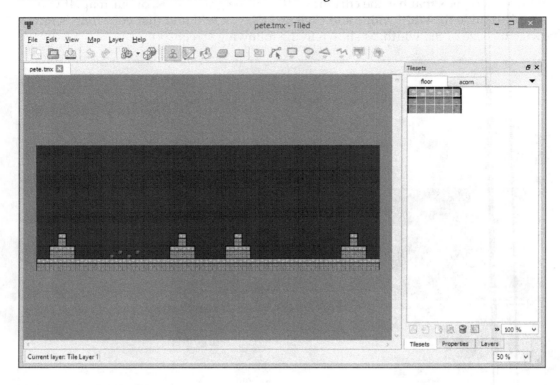

As you can see, this is a simple mirror image of what we already have.

If you try to run the project now, you will find that Pete is still constrained within the screen. He can't access the rest of the level! Let's fix this now.

Before we do this, let's just think about what we need to do here. We need to:

- Allow Pete to move off the screen
- Move the camera so that it follows Pete when he moves across the screen
- Stop Pete from wandering off at the end of the level!

Allowing Pete to leave the screen

First, let's tackle the problem of Pete moving off the screen. If we look at our `GameScreen` class again, we can see that we have a method called `stopPeteLeavingTheScreen()`. Here is the code for it in case you have forgotten:

```
private void stopPeteLeavingTheScreen() {
  if (pete.getY() < 0) {
    pete.setPosition(pete.getX(), 0);
    pete.landed();
  }
  if (pete.getX() < 0) {
    pete.setPosition(0, pete.getY());
  }
  if (pete.getX() + Pete.WIDTH > WORLD_WIDTH) {
    pete.setPosition(WORLD_WIDTH - Pete.WIDTH, pete.getY());
  }
}
```

We are interested in the last part of the code. Currently, we are saying that if the right-hand side of Pete (Pete's *x* coordinate plus his width) is greater than the width of the world, according to the camera, then we need to reset his position. However, we need to update the same as the level's width as well. So, let's update the method as follows:

```
private void stopPeteLeavingTheScreen() {
  if (pete.getY() < 0) {
    pete.setPosition(pete.getX(), 0);
    pete.landed();
  }
  if (pete.getX() < 0) {
    pete.setPosition(0, pete.getY());
  }
  TiledMapTileLayer tiledMapTileLayer = (TiledMapTileLayer)
  tiledMap.getLayers().get(0);
  float levelWidth =  tiledMapTileLayer.getWidth() *
  tiledMapTileLayer.getTileWidth();
  if (pete.getX() + Pete.WIDTH > levelWidth) {
    pete.setPosition(levelWidth - Pete.WIDTH, pete.getY());
  }
}
```

As you can see, we get a reference to the layer that we require. Then, we calculate the level's width and finally update the condition statement.

If you run the project now, you will find that you can make Pete go off the screen and come back.

Part one achieved! Next, we need to be able to move the camera.

The camera sees it all

Because we are only going to scroll to the left or right, we don't need to worry about updating the *y* axis of our camera. However, if you wanted up and down scrolling, what we will do here will apply to the *y* axis as well, for when the responsibility comes upon you to implement your own game.

Our first step is to create a method that will update the camera. In our `GameScreen` class, let's create a method called `updateCameraX()` — we will do this as we are only going to update the *x* coordinate.

You can see this method in the following code:

```
private void updateCameraX() {
  camera.position.set(pete.getX(), camera.position.y,
  camera.position.z);
  camera.update();
  orthogonalTiledMapRenderer.setView(camera);
}
```

Here, you can see that we are setting the position of the camera to be that of Pete's, updating the camera, and then updating the view on the `TileMapRenderer` parameter.

Next, we will add a call to this method in our `update()` method.

If you run the project now, you should hopefully see that the camera is centered around Pete on the *x* axis:

```
private void update(float delta) {
  pete.update(delta);
  stopPeteLeavingTheScreen();
  handlePeteCollision();
  handlePeteCollisionWithAcorn();
  updateCameraX();
}
```

However, you might have spotted the flaw in what we have just done. Let's look at the following image:

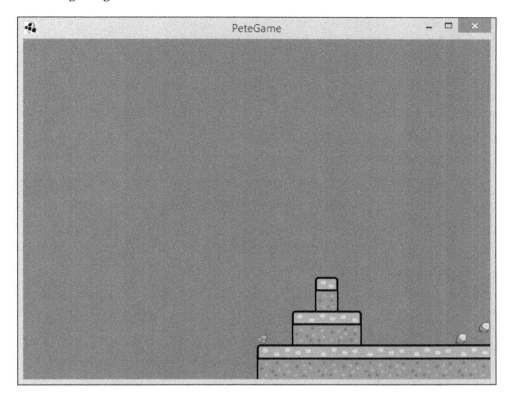

So, by centering the camera around Pete, we have exposed what is outside our level. In some games, this might actually be desirable. However, let's lock this position down so we don't expose what is happening in our game's behind-the-scenes!

To do this, we will need to update our `updateCameraX()` method to take into consideration Pete's position and only update the camera if he is in the middle of our level.

Update the method with the following code:

```
private void updateCameraX() {
  TiledMapTileLayer tiledMapTileLayer = (TiledMapTileLayer)
  tiledMap.getLayers().get(0);
  float levelWidth = tiledMapTileLayer.getWidth() *
  tiledMapTileLayer.getTileWidth();
  if ( (pete.getX() > WORLD_WIDTH / 2f) && (pete.getX() <
  (levelWidth - WORLD_WIDTH / 2f)) ) {
```

```
        camera.position.set(pete.getX(), camera.position.y,
        camera.position.z);
        camera.update();
        orthogonalTiledMapRenderer.setView(camera);
    }
}
```

So, once again, we retrieve the length of the level. We then check whether Pete is more than half in the screen width, but with not less than half a screen width remaining. We then update the camera.

If you run the project now, you will find that the camera is now bound to the level and will not go past either end. Let's take a look at the following screenshot:

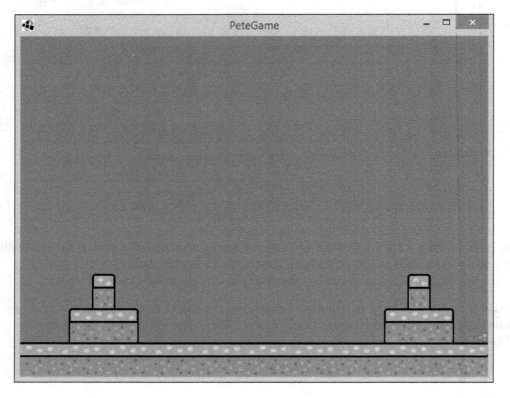

As you can see, Pete can't escape the end of the level and the camera has stopped scrolling.

Let's make some noise

So far, across all the games we have made, we can note that they all have something in common. They are completely silent! As any good game-maker knows, sounds and music add an awful lot to the experience. What we are going to look at now is how to use LibGDX to introduce sounds to our simple platform.

Before we dive into coding up some beeps and boops, let's first look at how LibGDX handles making sounds!

Sound effects

LibGDX splits the handling of audio into two parts. The first part is the sound effects with smaller audio files and the second part is the music, which generally has larger audio files. We will start off with looking at the `Sound` class of LibGDX, the one that looks after the smaller sound effects.

According to the LibGDX wiki (`https://github.com/libgdx/libgdx/wiki/Sound-effects`), the definition of which audio falls in the sound effects category is:

> *Sound effects are small audio samples, usually no longer than a few seconds, that are played back on specific game events such as a character jumping or shooting a gun.*

This fits in perfectly, as most sound effects we wish to use will be small, perhaps even less than a second in length.

In fact, I would strongly recommend that you read the LibGDX wiki, as it will provide you with more links for further reading.

LibGDX supports MP3, OGG, and WAV formats of audio files. Which format you use in your game will come down to many different decisions, such as how big the files can be, the level of quality of the audio required, and so on.

OK, so this is the background in which audios are classed as sound effects and formats are supported, but how do we play the sound once we have a background? As with the majority of things, with LibGDX, this is pleasingly simple. Those who have had a brief look at the wiki page will notice that the following line of code is pretty recognizable:

```
Sound sound = Gdx.audio.newSound
(Gdx.files.internal("data/mysound.mp3"));
```

Here, we load an MP3 audio file and generate an instance of the `Sound` interface class. You will recognize the file handle from the beginning of the book where we had loaded the textures in the same way. We pass this file handle to the audio class of the GDX object; this will then generate our instance.

Hey! You might be thinking "Why can't I just do something like what we did for the `Texture` class?"

```
Sound sound = new Sound(Gdx.files.internal("data/mysound.mp3"));
```

This is an excellent question. The answer should not really surprise you if you know a little bit about how LibGDX is cross-platform. For those who don't know, we will cover the cross-platform aspect in a later chapter. Now, back to the question at hand.

The `Gdx.audio` parameter will be platform-dependent, and games-makers will never explicitly set it. However, the implementation will be set by LibGDX for the platform that LibGDX runs on. This means that the `newSound()` method will contain an actual platform-dependent implementation. Thus, our `Sound` interface is required because our core code is platform agnostic.

Hopefully, this cleared everything up!

Right, now we have a handle on our audio, but how do we play it? Well, this again is pleasingly simple:

```
sound.play(1.0f);
```

This will play our sound at the full volume; the `1.0` value represents a ratio here. It will play our sound and then stop when it is finished and we can call this as many times as we like. There are more methods in the `Sound` class, but they are beyond the scope of what we want to do here. So, I again suggest you check out the wiki and reference guide on the LibGDX website for more information.

Finally, as with all the resources in the LibGDX world, once we are done with the audio, we need to dispose of it:

```
sound.dispose();
```

Music

Onto the game music now! Music in a game is a bit different than our sound effects, as we might want our music to last longer by perhaps a couple of minutes and then we would want it to be looped!

Since we saw that the `Sound` class is better for short audio clips, the `Music` class is suited to longer pieces.

The following definition is from the LibGDX music wiki (`https://github.com/libgdx/libgdx/wiki/Streaming-music`):

> *For any sound that's longer than a few seconds it is preferable to stream it from disk instead of fully loading it into RAM. LibGDX provides a Music interface that lets you do that.*

OK, so now we have our MP3 file that has the audio we wish to play. However, how do we play it? The following code shows us how this is possible:

```
Music music = Gdx.audio.newMusic(Gdx.files.internal
("data/mymusic.mp3"));
```

Doesn't this look a touch familiar? Well it should look very similar to the piece of code that we used before to load sounds. With a few exceptions, we will generate a `Music` implementation again as we did for the platform-dependent aspects of LibGDX; this is the reason why we are loading the music this way.

Once it is loaded, all we have to do is invoke the following code:

```
music.play()
```

There are other methods that can be called on the `Music` object, such as `setLooping()`, `setVolume()`, `stop()`, `pause()`, and others. We will come in contact with them when we add the sounds to our Pete the Platformer game.

As with the `Sound` class, we need to dispose of the object when we are done with it, as follows:

```
music.dispose()
```

It should be noted here that the `Music` instances are heavy weight objects and that keeping them to a minimum is advised.

In the final part, I will add the two types of audio classes that we have here. They can be cued up with the `AssetManager` parameter, which is awesome! This means that we won't have to know too much about where the audio comes from!

If Pete jumps in the game, does anyone hear him?

Now that we have the tools to add audio to our game, we should! What we will do now is go through the code and add two sound effects: one for the jump and one for the collectable pick-up. We will also use a music track that we will keep on playing.

Let's get down to the coding now!

First, we need to add our audio to the `AssetManager` parameter so that they will be loaded for us. There is actually a little side effect of sounds if they aren't loaded up in front as shown in the code, and this is usually manifested the first time you wish the audio to play; it won't, as it hasn't loaded yet.

In our `LoadingScreen` class, we should update the `show()` method to get the audio references:

```
public void show() {
    super.show();
    camera = new OrthographicCamera();
    camera.position.set(WORLD_WIDTH / 2, WORLD_HEIGHT / 2, 0);
    camera.update();
    viewport = new FitViewport(WORLD_WIDTH, WORLD_HEIGHT, camera);
    shapeRenderer = new ShapeRenderer();
    peteGame.getAssetManager().load("pete.png", Texture.class);
    peteGame.getAssetManager().load("acorn.png", Texture.class);
    peteGame.getAssetManager().load("pete.tmx", TiledMap.class);
    peteGame.getAssetManager().load("jump.wav", Sound.class);
    peteGame.getAssetManager().load("sacorn.wav", Sound.class);
    peteGame.getAssetManager().load("peteTheme.mp3", Music.class);
}
```

Quite simply, LibGDX will automatically know what to do with the code.

Next, let's get our sound effects going.

We have a jump sound effect and a sound effect for when Pete picks up an acorn. Let's focus on the jump sound effect to start with.

The first thing to achieve is to provide the `Pete` class a reference to the jump `Sound` object. Now, update the constructor of the class to take in a `Sound` object and assign it to a local variable:

```
private final Sound jumpSound;
public Pete(Texture texture, Sound jumpSound) {
    this.jumpSound = jumpSound;
    // Code omitted for brevity
}
```

This means that we now have access to the sound that we want inside the `Pete` class.

Next, we want to play this sound every time Pete jumps. To do this, we need to update the input handling code so that it plays the sound when the jump is initiated.

Update the `update()` method with the following code:

```
if (input.isKeyPressed(Input.Keys.UP) && !blockJump) {
  if (ySpeed != MAX_Y_SPEED) jumpSound.play();
  ySpeed = MAX_Y_SPEED;
  jumpYDistance += ySpeed;
  blockJump = jumpYDistance > MAX_JUMP_DISTANCE;
} else {
  ySpeed = -MAX_Y_SPEED;
  blockJump = jumpYDistance > 0;
}
```

Here, we are saying that if we are in the right conditions to jump and we haven't jumped yet (`ySpeed` parameter is not `MAX_Y_SPEED`), then the jump sound should be played.

The final piece of this puzzle is to update our instantiation of our `Pete` class in the `GameScreen` class to pass the `Sound` object:

```
public void show() {
  // Code omitted for brevity
  pete = new Pete(
    peteGame.getAssetManager().get("pete.png", Texture.class),
    peteGame.getAssetManager().get("jump.wav", Sound.class)
  );
  pete.setPosition(0, WORLD_HEIGHT / 2);
  populateAcorns();
}
```

Excellent; if you run the project now, you will find that we get a jump sound every time Pete jumps!

Our second sound, the collectable audio, needs to be played when Pete collides with an acorn. There is a very straightforward update to our `GameScreen` class that we need to make for this to happen. Let's update the `handlePeteCollisionWithAcorn()` method, as follows:

```
private void handlePeteCollisionWithAcorn() {
  for (Iterator<Acorn> iter = acorns.iterator(); iter.hasNext(); )
  {
    Acorn acorn = iter.next();
    if (pete.getCollisionRectangle().overlaps
    (acorn.getCollisionRectangle())) {
      peteGame.getAssetManager().get("acorn.wav",
      Sound.class).play();
```

```
        iter.remove();
      }
    }
  }
```

As you can see, when the two collide, we play the sound! If you run the project now, you will find that the audio is played when you pick up the acorn.

Our final task now is to get the music playing. Like the acorn pick-up sound effect, we can do this quite simply with one line of code. In our GameScreen class, let's update the show() method as follows:

```
public void show() {
  // Code omitted for brevity
  peteGame.getAssetManager().get("peteTheme.mp3",
  Music.class).play();
}
```

Now if you run the project, you will find that we have some background music as well!

However, you will find that the music stops when it comes to the end of the audio. This won't do; what if the player hasn't finished your level yet? Well, to fix this, we can add the following line of code before the play() method is invoked. So now, we end up with the following in our show() method:

```
peteGame.getAssetManager().get("peteTheme.mp3",
Music.class).setLooping(true);
peteGame.getAssetManager().get("peteTheme.mp3",
Music.class).play();
```

Aha! Now our music will loop forever!

Summary

Well, there we go. What a nice little chapter we had there!

We extended our level and scrolled the camera across the landscape. We successfully bounded the camera to the level so that we don't show any behind-the-scenes action to our players.

We then took our initial dive to play sounds with LibGDX that allowed us to have background music along with some awesome sound effects. This will really liven up your own games.

As with the previous game, there are some things that we didn't add to the game but we added to others, for example, a score. Here is a great opportunity for you to take what you have learned and apply it in Pete the Platformer!

In the next chapter, we will start a new game. This game is based on a well-known game about a bunch of pigs and very upset angry birds! We will look at how to apply some of the physics tools that LibGDX has. These will allow us to create a simple, but fun game!

8

Why Are All the Birds Angry?

Another new chapter and another new game! This time around we are going to be looking at making a simplified version of a modern-day mobile classic. That's right; we are going to have a look at Angry Birds.

For those that might be keen to see what this chapter will help you make, you can view a quick video of it at `https://www.youtube.com/watch?v=7Xot-5pkjIY`.

By choosing this game as a game to remake, we get the chance to look at some more advanced features of LibGDX, in particular the popular Box2D physics engine. Once again, we will be revisiting the great tool, that is, Tiled, for level creation and integration with Box2D, to simplify the design process.

To finish off, we will look at handling different types of input for the mouse (or finger, for mobiles) with actions such as drag. We will cover the following topics:

- The what, why, and how of Angry Birds
- Setting up a new project with Box2D
- Box2D with LibGDX
- Creating a world
- Nutty birds

The what, why, and how of Angry Birds

For our final game, we are looking at Angry Birds; for some, this will have been a staple game in your library since its launch in 2009. But just in case you have lived under a rock for the last few years, let's have a quick rundown on the game.

Angry Birds was first released on iPhones back in 2009, created by a company called Rovio. With around 2 billion downloads, it is one of the most popular games ever created.

From a gameplay perspective, the aim of the game is for the player to slingshot a bird, a very angry bird, into the enemy pigs' fortress. The idea is to eliminate all the pigs before the player runs out of birds to fling across the screen. The game mixes this action with a puzzle element as each fortress is differently designed with differing materials that require different attack tactics, and also there are different types of birds with different abilities that can be selected. Let's take a look at the following image:

The preceding is a screenshot of Angry Birds, showing a bird being flung into the enemy fortress.

Why?

The reason I chose Angry Birds as the game is partly due to its popularity but also because of a technical aspect with the introduction of Box2D. In fact, Box2D is the exact same technology Rovio used in Angry Birds, so it made sense. This also introduces the external dependency ability of LibGDX.

How?

LibGDX has this cool extension capability that allows you to add external libraries in a nice slick manner. Since Box2D is in essence a C/C++ library, it needs to be wrapped with some awesome Java Native wrapper code that funnily enough comes with the LibGDX extension. So, all the methods available natively will be available to us!

We will have Box2D for the physics, and then we will use Tiled for our level design. We then just have to glue it all together using LibGDX!

Setting up LibGDX with Box2D

Right, we need a LibGDX project that has Box2D support. The question is, how do we go ahead and create that? Well, the eagle-eyed among you will have noticed that Box2D was a selectable option in the project setup application we used previously and in fact it will have been already preselected!

The preceding partial screenshot of the setup application shows what you see when you rerun the application.

Set up the application like we have done so previously, but with Box2D ticked, and then we are good to go!

Code reuse

Next, before we dive into Box2D, let's reuse some code from our previous projects.

Firstly, we should update our NuttyGame class so it extends the Game class. This isn't something new, just look at our previous games!

Next, we can bring across our LoadingScreen class and create a simple GameScreen class. Don't worry about screen sizes for now, we will come to them later.

Hopefully, your game class will look like this:

```
public class NuttyGame extends Game {
  private final AssetManager assetManager = new AssetManager();

  @Override
  public void create() {
    setScreen(new LoadingScreen(this));
  }

  public AssetManager getAssetManager() {
    return assetManager;
  }
}
```

Looks familiar? It should, we have used this stuff before!

Box2D with LibGDX

Just before we jump into writing some code to make our new game, we should really cover the basics of Box2D so that we can get an understanding of what we are trying to achieve here.

Essentially, Box2D is a physics library and an extremely popular one at that.

It has its own website and I suggest you check it out. You can check it out at http://www.box2d.org, if you wish to get even more technical with its use—since we are just going to have a taster to start off with.

You might be wondering why am I directing you to their website when we are using LibGDX; well, as I mentioned before, LibGDX provides a thin Java wrapper to the native C++ library, so the API is going to be the same. Aren't those guys awesome?

For a more LibGDX-style approach, you can check out their awesome wiki. You should have guessed I was going to bring that up, right? They have a nice introduction to its use as well. You can find it at https://github.com/libgdx/libgdx/wiki/Box2d.

However, what we will do now is cover some Box2D terminology.

Box2D concepts

Box2D contains several different objects that can be used to simulate real-world physics. What I will do now is highlight the important ones. Like before, you can check the documentation to enhance your understanding. In fact, it is from the core concepts section that I have taken the following.

Shape

A shape is essentially a 2D geometrical object, such as a circle.

Rigid body

A rigid body is a chunk of matter so strong that the distance between any two bits of matter on the chunk is constant. You should think about this as a hard object, such as a diamond.

Fixture

A fixture maps a shape to a body and adds real-world material properties such as friction, restitution, and density. This also allows the shape to be recognized in the collision system.

Constraint

Every 2D body has three degrees of movement, essentially your x and y coordinates and one for rotation. A constraint allows you remove these, much like pinning a body to a wall, and it becomes like a pendulum.

The contact constraint

This is a special type of constraint that is used to prevent rigid bodies from penetrating one another, and it also simulates friction and restitution. You should note that Box2D will create these for us.

Joint

This is a type of constraint that is used to hold two or more bodies together. There are several different kinds/types of joint in the Box2D world.

The joint limit

This limits the range of motion of a joint.

The joint motor

This motor drives the motion of the connected bodies according to the degree of freedom.

World

This is an all-encompassing place where all the bodies, fixtures, and constraints interact together.

Solver

The world has one of these; they are used to advance time and resolve contact and joint constraints:

- Continuous collision
- The solver advances bodies in time using discrete time steps

Right, those were the concepts; hopefully, that is enough to get us going!

The final thing to discuss before writing some code will be units.

Units

Box2D works in a meters-kilogram-second (MKS) world. This means we shouldn't work in a pixel-based environment. But that's OK as we haven't since the early part of this book. Think of the `Viewport` class, for example. Now we need to think of everything in terms of meters, kilograms, and seconds. Considering the tuning that has gone into Box2D, they recommend moving shapes in the range of 0.1 to 10 meters. So, as they say in their documentation at `http://box2d.org/manual.pdf` `1.7 Units`:

> *"Box2D has been tuned to work well with moving shapes between 0.1 and 10 meters. So this means objects between soup cans and buses in size should work well. Static shapes may be up to 50 meters long without trouble."*

Just to back up the idea of not mapping 1 pixel to 1 meter, if you had a 64x 64-pixel sprite, that would translate to a 64 x 64 meter Box2D representation!

Oh! One last final, absolutely final thing. We will be working in radians not degrees!

Creating a world!

Excellent! Now we can dive into code and start creating a world. Once we have a world, we can look at populating it.

Firstly, we need to tell LibGDX to load the native libraries for Box2D. This is done with a simple static initialization call. Let's update the `create` method in our game class to do this:

```
public void create() {
  Box2D.init();
  setScreen(new LoadingScreen(this));
}
```

Good stuff! Now we are ready to create a world. If we didn't do this, we might run into some strange class-loading issues.

Next, let's create the world! We will need to define the following fields in our `GameScreen` class:

```
private static final float WORLD_WIDTH = 960;
private static final float WORLD_HEIGHT = 544;
private static final float UNITS_PER_METER = 16F;
private World world;
private Box2DDebugRenderer debugRenderer;
private Body body;
```

We have defined a world, debug renderer, and body. This body will just be used for a quick example before moving on. The units per meter will convert from our game world to the LibGDX world. This value will always vary depending on how you set your games up.

In our `show()` method, we need to instantiate our objects:

```
public void show() {
  world = new World(new Vector2(0, -10F), true);
  debugRenderer = new Box2DDebugRenderer();
  body = createBody();
  body.setTransform(100, 120, 0);
  camera = new OrthographicCamera();
  viewport = new FitViewport(WORLD_WIDTH, WORLD_HEIGHT, camera);
  viewport.apply(true);
  shapeRenderer = new ShapeRenderer();
}
```

Here we have created our world. We have defined some gravity, the Vector2 class, and we have zero impact in a horizontal plane but we have defined -10 on the vertical plane. This is to mimic real-world gravity—OK it should be 9.81m/s, but let's just keep it simple. We then create our debug renderer, and then create a body. Once we have this body, we set its position on screen. The Boolean flag defines whether we want to simulate inactive bodies, if we end up with too many bodes we can set this to False to improve performance.

To create a body, we will use the following code snippet:

```
private Body createBody() {
  BodyDef def = new BodyDef();
  def.type = BodyDef.BodyType.DynamicBody;
  Body box = world.createBody(def);
  PolygonShape poly = new PolygonShape();
  poly.setAsBox(60/UNITS_PER_METER, 60/UNITS_PER_METER);
  box.createFixture(poly, 1);
  poly.dispose();
  return box;
}
```

Here we first define the body definition; in this case it is going to be a dynamic rigid body, as it is going to move!

We then use the World object to create the body from the definition. Next we define the collision fixture. In this case, we are using PolygonShape that we are setting to a square. We create the fixture and then dispose of the shape. Finally, we return the body back.

Now, we need to tell the world to step through and update, otherwise nothing will happen:

```
private void update(float delta) {
  world.step(delta, 6, 2);
  body.setAwake(true);
}
```

Here we step through with the delta value as our time step—delta being the time between frames, and then we provide the velocity iterations and position iterations. You might be wondering why they are 6 and 2. Well, those who visited the LibGDX wiki will notice that these are the numbers they used, so we will just go with that for now. For more information on what effect those numbers have on the game, I suggest reading up on the Box2D documentation.

Our final step is to get the debug renderer to draw out what we have, which is a simple one line of code, in our `drawDebug()` method. Let's add the following:

```
debugRenderer.render(world, camera.combined);
```

With that all in place, if you run up the project, you should get the following:

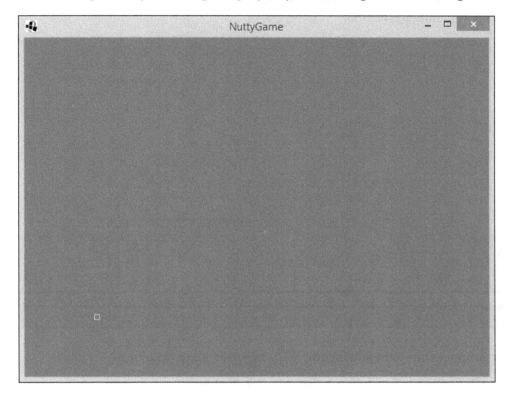

But not only that, the box should be falling down. If you leave it running, it will eventually disappear off the screen.

Yey! You have done your first Box2D coding. I know, I know, it isn't much. But it is a start!

Nutty Birds

Right, now is the time to introduce the game we are going to make ourselves. We shall call it Nutty Birds. We will follow the same gameplay as Angry Birds. Except, instead of flinging the birds at pigs, we will bring back our friend Pete the Squirrel and he will be lobbing his acorns at the birds—pesky birds living in his tree, probably stealing his acorns.

Here is a mock up of how the game will, hopefully, end up looking.

Pete will fling his acorn toward a simple fort. Perhaps this is level 1, where one of the naughty birds is hiding. As with Angry Birds, if the bird is hit with enough force, the pigs will disappear and the player will win the level.

Let's get tiling!

First things first, let's get the level screen set up. To do this, we are going to use that awesome tiling tool called Tiled again. However, this time we are going to do two, yes two! things with it.

I am going to assume that you are up to speed with how Tiled works so I am not going to go into too much detail on the setup as I did before.

The groundwork

To get started, create a new tile map and set it to be 30 x 17 tiles big with a tile size of 32 x 32 pixels.

Then, on the **Layers** tab, rename the tiled layer to `Ground`, and then add a new layer, but this time choose the image layer! The image layer is, simply put, a layer that is represented by an image—perfect for our background. Call this layer `Background` and then make sure it is at the bottom of the list—since it is at the back. Your layers pane should look like this:

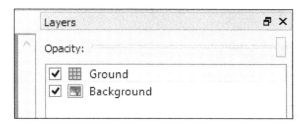

Next, with the **Background** layer highlighted. Click on **Properties**—at the bottom there—and you will see the properties of the image layer. One of the properties you will notice is **Image**; if you click on it, you will have the option to add an image. It should end up looking like this:

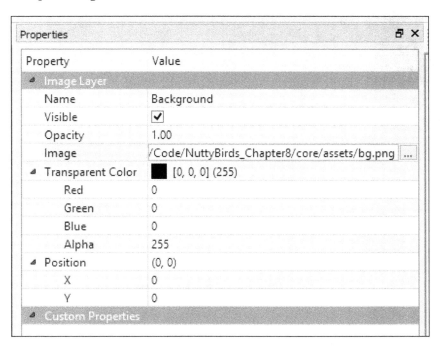

Note that your project location might/will/could/would/should be a different location to mine.

Hopefully, this will now have the background image appear in the main window, as shown in the following screenshot:

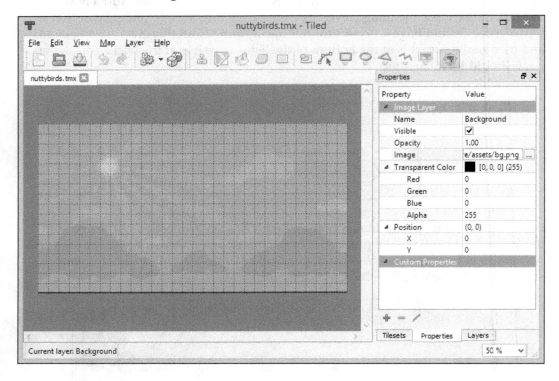

Continuing on, we need to add the tile set to the tiled layer so that we can add the floor. Head back to the **Layers** tab and select the **Ground** layer, and then click back onto the **Tilesets** tab and add the floor image to the tile set. Finally, grab the stamping tool and build a floor that is two-tiles high, as shown in the following screenshot:

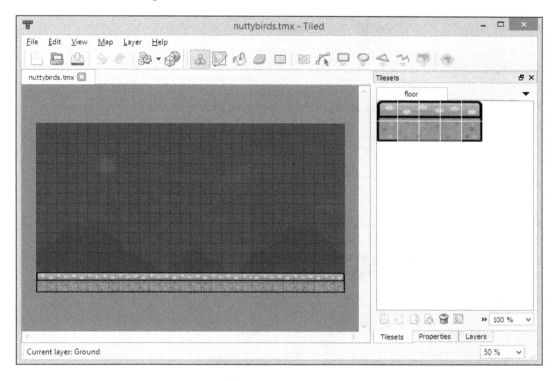

That's the groundwork done. However, what we need to do is lay out the physics items; luckily this is something Tiled can help us achieve.

Adding objects

To have Tiled help us achieve easy placing of our physic bodies, we need to add a layer known as an Object Layer. This will allow us to draw shapes that we can then import into our game and build Box2D bodies from.

So, go back to your **Layers** tab and add a new object layer—call it `Physics_Buildings` and ensure it is at the top of the list, as shown in the following screenshot:

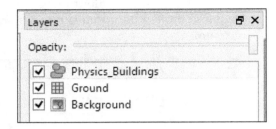

With that layer selected, we can use the shapes tools from the toolbar, as shown in the next screenshot:

With Square selected, we need to draw out four boxes similar to the positions I have them in the following screenshot. You should note that you will need to start from the top-left corner and drag to the bottom-right corner. To make this easier, we can also turn on **Snap to Grid** under the **View** menu.

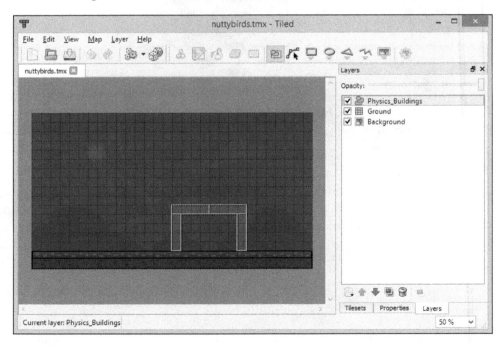

Perfect, but this won't do much at the moment as we don't handle it yet in code. Our next step is to add another object layer—called `Physics_Birds`—so that we can place our naughty bird. The steps will be the same as earlier, but this time use the Circle tool for the bird. We will use a circle as we will want the bird to roll when it gets struck by the building parts.

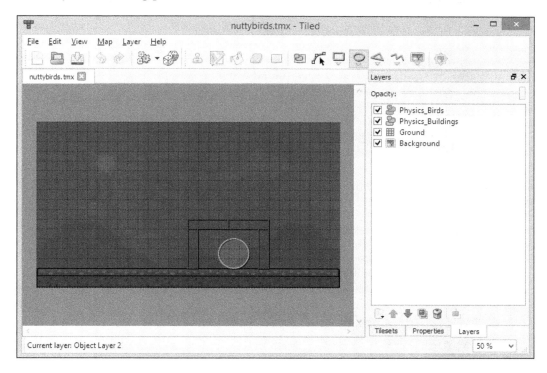

Excellent! Looks like we can have a go now at importing it in to our game!

Importing the tile map

Now we need to actually write some code! Or rather, we must first delete some. Let's remove the body we created to show a quick example of Box2D in action.

Next, we need to add the code that handles the tile map. I am not going to go into too much detail here as this is something we have covered previously.

Firstly, remember to add the required loader to the `AssetManager` class in our game class:

```
public void create() {
  Box2D.init();
  assetManager.setLoader(TiledMap.class, new TmxMapLoader(new
  InternalFileHandleResolver()));
  setScreen(new LoadingScreen(this));
}
```

Next, update our `LoadingScreen` class to load our Tiled map:

```
public void show() {
  // Code omitted for brevity
  nuttyGame.getAssetManager().load("nuttybirds.tmx",
  TiledMap.class);
}
```

Finally, we need to update our `GameScreen` class with the code that will load and display our Tiled map.

Remember, we need to define the following:

```
private SpriteBatch batch;
private TiledMap tiledMap;
private OrthogonalTiledMapRenderer orthogonalTiledMapRenderer;
```

Then, instantiate them in the `show()` method:

```
tiledMap = nuttyGame.getAssetManager().get("nuttybirds.tmx");
orthogonalTiledMapRenderer = new OrthogonalTiledMapRenderer(tiledMap,
batch);
orthogonalTiledMapRenderer.setView(camera);
```

Finally, update the `draw()` method to render the map:

```
private void draw() {
  batch.setProjectionMatrix(camera.projection);
  batch.setTransformMatrix(camera.view);
  orthogonalTiledMapRenderer.render();
}
```

Hopefully, with all this in place, when you run the project, you should get the following output:

This is just what we want. Next, we will import the object maps and create our Box2D bodies from the objects.

Importing the object layer

Our next task is to take the object layer for the building parts and generate bodies for them. We will create a new class `TiledObjectBodyBuilder`, and in here we will have a static method that we pass our `TiledMap` and `World` classes to:

```
public class TiledObjectBodyBuilder {
  private static final float PIXELS_PER_TILE = 32F;
  private static final float HALF = 0.5F;
  public static void buildBuildingBodies(TiledMap tiledMap, World
  world) {
    MapObjects objects =
    tiledMap.getLayers().get("Physics_Buildings").getObjects();
    for (MapObject object : objects) {
      PolygonShape rectangle = getRectangle((RectangleMapObject)
      object);
      BodyDef bd = new BodyDef();
```

```
            bd.type = BodyDef.BodyType.DynamicBody;
            Body body = world.createBody(bd);
            body.createFixture(rectangle, 1);
            rectangle.dispose();
        }
    }

    private static PolygonShape getRectangle(RectangleMapObject
    rectangleObject) {
        Rectangle rectangle = rectangleObject.getRectangle();
        PolygonShape polygon = new PolygonShape();
        Vector2 size = new Vector2(
            (rectangle.x + rectangle.width * HALF) / PIXELS_PER_TILE,
            (rectangle.y + rectangle.height * HALF) / PIXELS_PER_TILE
        );
        polygon.setAsBox(
            rectangle.width * HALF / PIXELS_PER_TILE,
            rectangle.height * HALF / PIXELS_PER_TILE,
            size,
            0.0f);
        return polygon;
    }
}
```

The preceding code listing is for the builder class. Let's go through this, break it down, and get an understanding of what we are doing here.

First we define how big our tiles are in pixels, which in this case is 32:

```
private static final float PIXELS_PER_TILE = 32F;
```

We then have a constant just to reduce the amount of magic numbers in the code.

Next we have the method that does all the hard work. Firstly, it obtains the layer that we require from the map and then the associated objects:

```
MapObjects objects = tiledMap.getLayers().get("Physics_Buildings").
getObjects();
```

Here we have an iterable class that contains all the objects in our layer.

Next, we iterate over those objects and we create a `PolygonShape` instance, similar to our previous example:

```
for (MapObject object : objects) {
  PolygonShape rectangle = getRectangle((RectangleMapObject)
  object);
  BodyDef bd = new BodyDef();
  bd.type = BodyDef.BodyType.DynamicBody;
  Body body = world.createBody(bd);
  body.createFixture(rectangle, 1);
  rectangle.dispose();
}
```

But here we are using the position and size of the object from the Tiled map to position our shapes in the Box2D world. We create the required fixture, so it enters the collision system of Box2D. Finally, we dispose off the shape and we are good to go.

Now that we have that handy class, let's add a call to it in our `GameScreen` class. We shall add the following code to the `show()` method:

```
TiledObjectBodyBuilder.buildBuildingBodies(tiledMap, world);
```

Excellent! Now run up the project and let's see what happens.

Ah ha! We have a problem here. You may or may not see anything; if you did, I bet it was really tiny and in the corner. Well, this is because we need to update our debug renderer for Box2D to work from a different camera as its meters are different from our world units.

To do this, let's add the following constants:

```
private static float UNITS_PER_METER = 32F;
private static float UNIT_WIDTH = WORLD_WIDTH / UNITS_PER_METER;
private static float UNIT_HEIGHT = WORLD_HEIGHT / UNITS_PER_METER;
```

Here we are creating a conversion to the world of Box2D from our world units. Again, we are using 32 because it is the size of our tiles.

Next, we need to define a new camera:

```
private OrthographicCamera box2dCam;
```

Instantiate it with our new constants. The following code is added to the `show()` method:

```
box2dCam = new OrthographicCamera(UNIT_WIDTH, UNIT_HEIGHT);
```

Then, in our `update()` method, we need to set the position and update the camera:

```
box2dCam.position.set(UNIT_WIDTH / 2, UNIT_HEIGHT / 2, 0);
box2dCam.update();
```

Finally, let's update the `drawDebug()` method to work with the new camera:

```
debugRenderer.render(world, box2dCam.combined);
```

Perfect! Now, if we run the project, we should have the following:

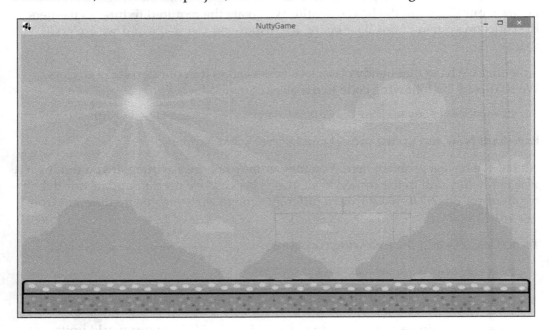

Oh no! Another problem! Even though they load correctly, we don't have a ground, so they just fall out of the screen and on to infinity! Looks like we should add a static body that will be our floor. Back to Tiled we go!

A world without floors.

OK, this will be simple to fix, and, in fact, I bet you have already steamed ahead, created another layer in Tiled, called it `Physics_Floor`, and added a rectangle to be the floor!

No? OK not a problem, let's do it together.

Create a new object layer called `Physics_Floor` and position it such that it is between the buildings and ground layers, as shown in the following screenshot:

Next, using the Rectangle tool, create a rectangle that covers the bottom two tiles. So it will end up like this:

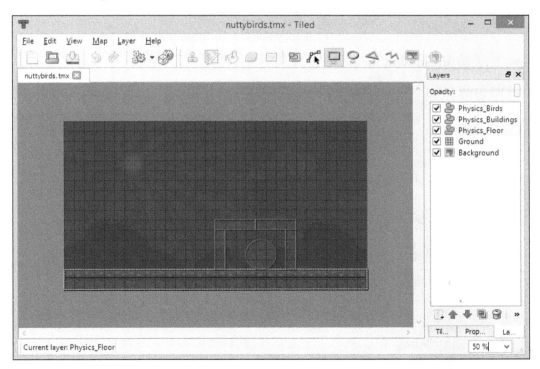

Excellent! Now back to the code to handle this floor. What we can do is create a new method in our builder class and have it exclusively handle floor components as follows:

```
public static void buildFloorBodies(TiledMap tiledMap, World world) {
  MapObjects objects =
  tiledMap.getLayers().get("Physics_Floor").getObjects();
  for (MapObject object : objects) {
    PolygonShape rectangle = getRectangle((RectangleMapObject)
    object);
    BodyDef bd = new BodyDef();
    bd.type = BodyDef.BodyType.StaticBody;
    Body body = world.createBody(bd);
    body.createFixture(rectangle, 1);
    rectangle.dispose();
  }
}
```

Now, update the GameScreen class to call this method, from within the shcw() method, just above our other build call:

```
TiledObjectBodyBuilder.buildFloorBodies(tiledMap, world);
```

Now let's go ahead with the project!

Yes!!!! Oh no, stop, wait, nooooooooooooooooooo....

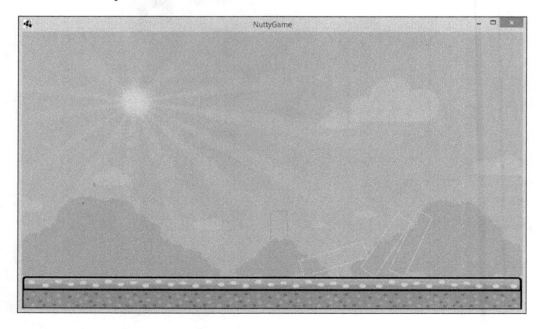

Did your build collapse like mine? Well, I guess it didn't fall off the screen.

Well, I suggest we fiddle with our building design! If we move the posts in a bit, it should all support itself, go back to Tiled, and have a go at moving your objects. This will be good practice when you come to making your own levels!

Here is what I came up with!

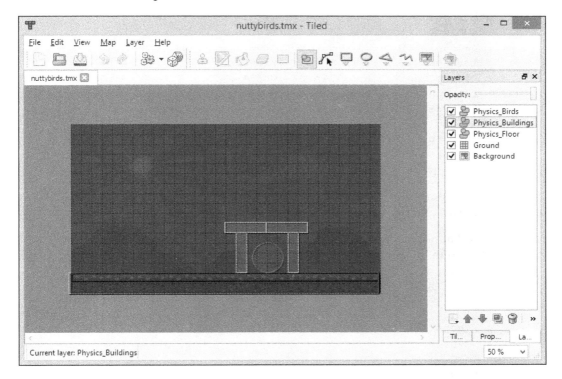

If you try that, you will find it supports itself!

Now, we just need to import the circle for the bird and we have that part complete— complete in the physics sense!

Importing the naughty ones!

Yey, well done on making it this far. I hope you are having fun seeing the physics in action! I know I am.

Now, to import the enemy birds, we need to update our builder to support circle physics shapes. Let's start there, and add the following code to that class:

```
private static CircleShape getCircle(EllipseMapObject
ellipseObject) {
  Ellipse ellipse = ellipseObject.getEllipse();
  CircleShape circleShape = new CircleShape();
  circleShape.setRadius(ellipse.width * HALF / PIXELS_PER_TILE);
  circleShape.setPosition(new Vector2((ellipse.x + ellipse.width *
  HALF) / PIXELS_PER_TILE, (ellipse.y + ellipse.height * HALF) /
  PIXELS_PER_TILE));
  return circleShape;
}
```

In the Tiled world, it isn't a circle it is an ellipse, but since we want a circle in the Box2D world, we need to do some extra code work. Here, we take the ellipse object and create a circle shape.

Next, we need a method that will call this one and iterate over all the enemies that might be in that layer. The following is the code that needs to be added to the builder class:

```
public static void buildBirdBodies(TiledMap tiledMap, World world)
{
  MapObjects objects =
  tiledMap.getLayers().get("Physics_Birds").getObjects();
  for (MapObject object : objects) {
    CircleShape circle = getCircle((EllipseMapObject) object);
    BodyDef bd = new BodyDef();
    bd.type = BodyDef.BodyType.DynamicBody;
    Body body = world.createBody(bd);
    body.createFixture(circle, 1);
    circle.dispose();
  }
}
```

You will notice it is very, very similar to the others.

Finally, add a call to this method in the show() method of the GameScreen class and we should be good to go!

```
TiledObjectBodyBuilder.buildBirdBodies(tiledMap, world);
```

Run that project and you will see the following:

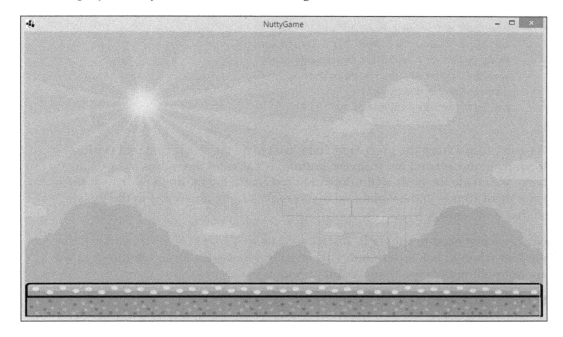

Excellent! In physics form, we have our enemy, that naughty acorn stealing bird, and the building protecting him.

Moving on, we will now need to handle the acorn and have it thrown in to the building, making it collapse!

Fire at will!

Moving on, we need to now provide something that will hit the building and hopefully knock it down!

To do this, we will need another body. We will again use the circle shape and, just to start with, we will have it fire when you click on the screen.

Let's create a method called `createBullet()` in our `GameScreen` class. In this class, will create a circular body and give some initial velocity:

```
private void createBullet() {
  CircleShape circleShape = new CircleShape();
  circleShape.setRadius(0.5f);
  circleShape.setPosition(new Vector2(3,6));
  BodyDef bd = new BodyDef();
  bd.type = BodyDef.BodyType.DynamicBody;
  Body bullet = world.createBody(bd);
  bullet.createFixture(circleShape, 0);
  circleShape.dispose();
  bullet.setLinearVelocity(10,6);
}
```

As you can see from the preceding code, we create the shape first and position it 3m from the left and 6m from the bottom, we also set the radius to be 0.5m. Next, we create the body definition and then create the fixture. Finally, we set a velocity of 10m/s in the x plane so that it moves right, and 6m/s in the y plane so that it moves up.

Now, we just need to trigger it. To this we can set `InputProcessor` and call the method when a click is detected. This is using event-style input handling, as we are not polling the input like we did previously.

In our `show()` method, let's add the following code:

```
Gdx.input.setInputProcessor(new InputAdapter() {
  @Override
  public boolean touchDown(int screenX, int screenY, int pointer,
  int button) {
    createBullet();
    return true;
  }
});
```

Here we create an instance of an anonymous class called `InputAdapter`. This class has a few interesting methods, but for now we are only interested in the `touchDown()` method. In this method, we call our `createBullet()`. Finally, that is set on the `Gdx.input` class, effectively telling LibGDX that we want to handle this input.

Excellent! If we fire up the project now and start clicking on the screen. You should see lots of bullets flying toward and hopefully knocking down the building.

As you can see, I got a little carried away there! But hey it works! We almost have a game here.

To make it a game, we are going to need to detect any force that occurs on the enemies so that we can decide whether it was enough to defeat them.

But I hardly touched him!

One of the many great things about Box2D is its collision handling. Now, we can see all the collisions happen on screen and we can mentally work out what should happen; however, when it comes to a computer working this out, there aren't enough CPU cycles to go around; obviously, this depends on how many bodies are flying around the screen!

So, to save CPU cycles, Box2D does a couple of cool things. Firstly, it will check collisions based on a technique using **Axis Aligned Bounding Box (AABB)**, where each object had a rectangular box over it, even if it is a circle! If these overlay, then it will dive deeper into where fixtures overlap and how to resolve them. This high-level collision detection is commonly known as the broad phase and is relatively cheap to calculate. In fact, we did something similar in the previous game.

Once it knows which fixtures potentially collide, Box2D can go on to the next phase called the narrow phase. In this phase, it will look at each contact in depth and calculate the best way to resolve this collision.

Thankfully, because Box2D takes care of all this for us, as you probably noticed when you were firing your bullets at the building, we don't need to go into great detail. The part we are interested in is the `ContactListener` class. This interface has various callbacks for the state of a collision. The following is the API:

```
public interface ContactListener {
    public void beginContact (Contact contact);
    public void endContact (Contact contact);
    public void preSolve (Contact contact, Manifold oldManifold);
    public void postSolve (Contact contact, ContactImpulse impulse);
}
```

It is pretty straightforward. The first two methods are for when the contact between two fixtures starts and ends, and the other two methods are for before and after the solver has done its work and repositioned the fixtures. We are only going to be interested in the `beginContact()` method. But please, feel free to read more about this in the Box2D documentation.

Back to the code! We want to create our own implementation of the `ContactListener` interface. Create this as an inner class in the `GameScreen` class for now, I called it `NuttyContactListener`.

Now for some code, in the `beginContact()` method, let's have the following:

```
if (contact.isTouching()) {
  Fixture attacker = contact.getFixtureA();
  Fixture defender = contact.getFixtureB();
  WorldManifold worldManifold = contact.getWorldManifold();
  if ("enemy".equals(defender.getUserData())) {
    Vector2 vel1 = attacker.getBody().
    getLinearVelocityFromWorldPoint(worldManifold.getPoints()[0]);
    Vector2 vel2 = defender.getBody().
    getLinearVelocityFromWorldPoint(worldManifold.getPoints()[0]);
    Vector2 impactVelocity = vel1.sub(vel2);
    if (Math.abs(impactVelocity.x) > 1 ||
    Math.abs(impactVelocity.y) > 1) {
      toRemove.add(defender.getBody());
    }
  }
}
```

Ah ha! The first line is going to be a bit confusing—shouldn't they already be touching? Well, their AABBs are touching but the actual fixtures might not be. Think about the square and the circle shapes. So, with us deciding that the fixtures are definitely touching, we can extract the fixtures from the Contact class. We also extract something called WorldManifold. This essentially contains the line between two contacting fixtures; we will need this later. Next, we check to see if the second fixture, the defender, is the enemy. We do this by looking at the user data we will add to the fixture and seeing if it equates to the literal enemy string. If that is the case, we now need to work out how strong the contact was when they collided, and we do this by getting the velocities at those points and subtracting one from the other. Finally, if either the x or y component is over an arbitrary value, I picked 1 but you can choose whatever feels right in the game, too high and you might not defeat the enemy. We add the body to an array to remove at a later time. Box2D doesn't like you removing bodies from the world at the wrong time, since this can cause a fatal error and crash.

Phew! I hope that makes sense so far. You will probably have a couple of errors at the moment as we haven't defined our array. So let's add that to the GameScreen class:

```
private Array<Body> toRemove = new Array<>();
```

Now, we need a method to remove the bodies that we wish to destroy:

```
private void clearDeadBodies() {
  for (Body body : toRemove) {
    world.destroyBody(body);
  }
  toRemove.clear();
}
```

Then, add it to our update() method:

```
private void update(float delta) {
  clearDeadBodies();
  world.step(delta, 6, 2);
  box2dCam.position.set(UNIT_WIDTH / 2, UNIT_HEIGHT / 2, 0);
  box2dCam.update();
}
```

Excellent! Now, when the naughty birds are hit and hurt, they will be removed from the physics world.

Finally, we just need to set our contact listener. So, in the `show()` method, add the following line:

```
world.setContactListener(new NuttyContactListener());
```

Super! Oh! One other final thing, we need to set the user data for our enemy. Back to our `TiledObjectBodyBuilder` class we go, and in our `buildBirdBodies()` method, we need to update the `createFixture()` method call to assign a local reference we then use:

```
Fixture fixture = body.createFixture(circle, 1);
```

Now, we can add the following line before we dispose of our circle:

```
fixture.setUserData("enemy");
```

Now, we should be good to go. If you run the project and start hurling those projectiles at the building, it should collapse and wipe out that circle!

As you can see from the preceding screenshot, the circle is gone! Just what we wanted.

The last thing we need to do before we start adding more artwork is to handle the firing mechanism.

Take Aim! Fire!

Right, now we are building what is essentially the catapult part. The way we are going to approach this is, we are going to define a point in the game world that will be our anchor point, and then we will have a point that is continually updated by the mouse cursor. From those two points, we will be able to derive an angle and how strongly to throw the acorn.

Let's start by first defining some variables that we will use. Once again in our `GameScreen` class, define the following:

```
private static final float MAX_STRENGTH = 15;
private static final float MAX_DISTANCE = 100;
private static final float UPPER_ANGLE = 3 * MathUtils.PI / 2f;
private static final float LOWER_ANGLE = MathUtils.PI / 2f;

private final Vector2 anchor = new
Vector2(convertMetresToUnits(3), convertMetresToUnits(6));
private final Vector2 firingPosition = anchor.cpy();
private float distance;
private float angle;
```

Here we have a few constants that will define some boundaries for our catapult; remember, we are working in radians here. Next, we define our anchor point and a field to keep track of our firing position. Finally, we define two fields to look after the distance and angle of our catapult.

I have also added two methods that you will need, and which will allow us to convert from Box2D meters to our world units:

```
private float convertUnitsToMetres(float pixels) {
  return pixels / UNITS_PER_METER;
}

private float convertMetresToUnits(float metres) {
  return metres * UNITS_PER_METER;
}
```

These will come in handy when we start to put our art in.

Next up is a bit of mathematical work to help us calculate two things. Firstly, the angle between two points:

```java
private float angleBetweenTwoPoints() {
    float angle = MathUtils.atan2(anchor.y - firingPosition.y,
    anchor.x - firingPosition.x);
    angle %= 2 * MathUtils.PI;
    if (angle < 0) angle += 2 * MathUtils .PI2;
    return angle;
}
```

Here we use the arctan method of the Java Math utils class with the difference in position between our two points, which are the anchor and the firing position. Then, we just bound the angle so that it will always appear between 0 and 2*Pi (0 to 360 degrees).

Our second method is for finding the distance between the two points:

```java
private float distanceBetweenTwoPoints() {
    return (float) Math.sqrt(((anchor.x - firingPosition.x) *
    (anchor.x - firingPosition.x)) + ((anchor.y - firingPosition.y)
    * (anchor.y - firingPosition.y)));
}
```

Perhaps you can figure out which mathematical method is being used here.

With all this information at hand, we can tie it all together with a method that will take the location of the mouse and tell us the distance—which will be the power— and the angle. We will use the angle to distribute the power between the x and the y planes.

Add the following code to your `GameScreen` class:

```java
private void calculateAngleAndDistanceForBullet(int screenX, int
screenY) {
    firingPosition.set(screenX, screenY);
    viewport.unproject(firingPosition);
    distance = distanceBetweenTwoPoints();
    angle = angleBetweenTwoPoints();
    if (distance > MAX_DISTANCE) {
        distance = MAX_DISTANCE;
    }
    if (angle > LOWER_ANGLE) {
        if (angle > UPPER_ANGLE) {
            angle = 0;
        } else {
```

```
            angle = LOWER_ANGLE;
        }
    }
    firingPosition.set(anchor.x +  (distance * -
    MathUtils.cos(angle)), anchor.y +  (distance * -
    MathUtils.sin(angle)));
}
```

Let's see what we have here. Firstly, we take the screen coordinates and unproject them against our viewport. This converts them from the real-world to our game-world units. Next up, we call our two mathematical methods before setting some boundaries up so that we cap the distance at the maximum, and the same with the angle. Finally, we reset the position of the firing position variable as it might currently be outside the boundary.

The next step related to changes we have to make involves updating the input processor. We now no longer want to fire a bullet (or acorn) on `touchDown()`, so we can do away with that. Instead, we are going to trigger the bullet creation on `touchUp()` and call our distance and angle calculating method in the `touchDragged()` method. Go ahead and update the `InputAdapter` as follows:

```
Gdx.input.setInputProcessor(new InputAdapter() {
  @Override
  public boolean touchDragged(int screenX, int screenY, int
  pointer) {
    calculateAngleAndDistanceForBullet(screenX, screenY);
    return true;
  }

  @Override
  public boolean touchUp(int screenX, int screenY, int pointer,
  int button) {
    createBullet();
    firingPosition.set(anchor.cpy());
    return true;
  }
});
```

As a final touch, we reset the position of the firing point.

Now, with that in place, we should update our `createBullet()` method using the distance and the angle we provide. Here is how the code now looks:

```
private void createBullet() {
  CircleShape circleShape = new CircleShape();
  circleShape.setRadius(0.5f);
```

```
        circleShape.setPosition(new
        Vector2(convertUnitsToMetres(firingPosition.x),
        convertUnitsToMetres(firingPosition.y)));
        BodyDef bd = new BodyDef();
        bd.type = BodyDef.BodyType.DynamicBody;
        Body bullet = world.createBody(bd);
        bullet.createFixture(circleShape, 1);
        circleShape.dispose();
        float velX = Math.abs( (MAX_STRENGTH * -MathUtils.cos(angle) *
        (distance / 100f)));
        float velY = Math.abs( (MAX_STRENGTH * -MathUtils.sin(angle) *
        (distance / 100f)));
        bullet.setLinearVelocity(velX, velY);
    }
```

A few things to note here. Firstly, we are now setting the initial position to be that of the firing point. Next, when we create the fixture, we give the bullet a density of 1; this will allow it to rotate and roll around on the static floor. Finally, we do some more mathematical gymnastics to calculate our x and y velocities. As you can see, they are the ratio of the angle and distance.

Our final step is to just get the debug shape renderer to display our two points and the line. I have updated the `drawDebug()` method as follows:

```
private void drawDebug() {
    debugRenderer.render(world, box2dCam.combined);
    shapeRenderer.setProjectionMatrix(camera.projection);
    shapeRenderer.setTransformMatrix(camera.view);
    shapeRenderer.begin(ShapeRenderer.ShapeType.Line);
    shapeRenderer.rect(anchor.x - 5, anchor.y - 5, 10, 10);
    shapeRenderer.rect(firingPosition.x - 5, firingPosition.y - 5,
    10, 10);
    shapeRenderer.line(anchor.x, anchor.y, firingPosition.x,
    firingPosition.y);
    shapeRenderer.end();
}
```

We should be all set, run up the project, and let's see what happens.

Hopefully, when you click and drag, you will have something similar to the preceding screenshot. When released, it should cause our projectile to fly through the air. Give it a go at different angles. You should notice you can't extend the line too far and it is bounded by the angles.

Our final step before we are finished here is to add the art assets in.

Time for an art attack!

Here we are at the final part we are going to cover. You might be thinking "Well, we have covered this earlier in the book, I know how to add textures to a game. What could you possibly show me now?"

Well, my intrepid reader, having a texture follow the position of a Box2D isn't as straightforward as you would like to think it is. We have to make some changes to the code we use to build our scene.

So, first up, let's dive into some code and update our `TiledObjectBodyBuilder` class. We need to update this class because the problem we have is that we position the fixture relative to the body, and currently all our bodies are at 0,0 but our fixtures are placed where we would expect them to be. If we move our bodies to where the fixtures are but don't update the code, they will be positioned relative to that new position and thus not be where we want them to be.

With that in mind, first we should update the `getRectangle()` and `getCircle()` methods to remove the setting of the fixture position, as follows:

```
private static PolygonShape getRectangle(RectangleMapObject
rectangleObject) {
  Rectangle rectangle = rectangleObject.getRectangle();
  PolygonShape polygon = new PolygonShape();
  polygon.setAsBox(rectangle.width * HALF / PIXELS_PER_TILE,
  rectangle.height * HALF / PIXELS_PER_TILE);
  return polygon;
}
private static CircleShape getCircle(EllipseMapObject
ellipseObject) {
  Ellipse ellipse = ellipseObject.getEllipse();
  CircleShape circleShape = new CircleShape();
  circleShape.setRadius(ellipse.width * HALF / PIXELS_PER_TILE);
  return circleShape;
}
```

Next, we are going to add a little helper method to get the position of a rectangle from the `RectangleMapObject` class, suitable to be used with a Box2D body. The following is the code:

```
private static Vector2 getTransformForRectangle(Rectangle
rectangle) {
  return new Vector2((rectangle.x + (rectangle.width * HALF)) /
  PIXELS_PER_TILE, (rectangle.y + (rectangle.height * HALF)) /
  PIXELS_PER_TILE);
}
```

Nothing scary or new there. When setting the position of a body, we need to place it by the center point, hence the half width and half height.

Now we can update the rest of the class to use this new method and to place our bodies and not the fixtures.

The following code shows the three methods in all their glory:

```java
public static void buildBirdBodies(TiledMap tiledMap, World world)
{
  MapObjects objects = tiledMap.getLayers().
  get("Physics_Birds").getObjects();

  for (MapObject object : objects) {
    EllipseMapObject ellipseMapObject = (EllipseMapObject) object;
    CircleShape circle = getCircle(ellipseMapObject);
    BodyDef bd = new BodyDef();
    bd.type = BodyDef.BodyType.DynamicBody;
    Body body = world.createBody(bd);
    Fixture fixture = body.createFixture(circle, 1);
    fixture.setUserData("enemy");
    body.setUserData("enemy");

    Ellipse ellipse = ellipseMapObject.getEllipse();
    body.setTransform(new Vector2((ellipse.x + ellipse.width *
    HALF) / PIXELS_PER_TILE, (ellipse.y + ellipse.height * HALF) /
    PIXELS_PER_TILE), 0);
    circle.dispose();
  }
}

public static void buildBuildingBodies(TiledMap tiledMap, World
world) {
  MapObjects objects =
  tiledMap.getLayers().get("Physics_Buildings").getObjects();

  for (MapObject object : objects) {
    RectangleMapObject rectangleMapObject = (RectangleMapObject)
    object;
    PolygonShape rectangle = getRectangle(rectangleMapObject);
    BodyDef bd = new BodyDef();
    bd.type = BodyDef.BodyType.DynamicBody;
    Body body = world.createBody(bd);

    if (rectangleMapObject.getRectangle().width >
    rectangleMapObject.getRectangle().height) {
      body.setUserData("horizontal");
    } else {
```

```
            body.setUserData("vertical");
      }

      body.createFixture(rectangle, 1);
      body.setTransform(getTransformForRectangle
      (rectangleMapObject.getRectangle()), 0);
      rectangle.dispose();
    }
  }

  public static void buildFloorBodies(TiledMap tiledMap, World
  world) {
    MapObjects objects = tiledMap.getLayers().get
    ("Physics_Floor").getObjects();

    for (MapObject object : objects) {
      RectangleMapObject rectangleMapObject = (RectangleMapObject)
      object;
      PolygonShape rectangle = getRectangle(rectangleMapObject);
      BodyDef bd = new BodyDef();
      bd.type = BodyDef.BodyType.StaticBody;
      Body body = world.createBody(bd);
      body.setUserData("floor");
      body.createFixture(rectangle, 1);
      body.setTransform(getTransformForRectangle
      (rectangleMapObject.getRectangle()), 0);
      rectangle.dispose();
    }
  }
```

As you can see, we are using the setTransform() method of our bodies; this means we can now position textures relative to that.

Hopefully, you will have spotted the other tiny addition in the preceding code. By setting the user data of each body to have a name, we can query the world for bodies later on and decide which textures to use.

Before we use our textures, we must make sure we load them. In our LoadingScreen class, we shall now update our show() method to add the additional textures:

```
public void show() {
  // Code omitted for brevity
  nuttyGame.getAssetManager().load("obstacleVertical.png",
  Texture.class);
  nuttyGame.getAssetManager().load("obstacleHorizontal.png",
  Texture.class);
```

```
nuttyGame.getAssetManager().load("bird.png", Texture.class);
nuttyGame.getAssetManager().load("slingshot.png",
Texture.class);
nuttyGame.getAssetManager().load("squirrel.png", Texture.class);
nuttyGame.getAssetManager().load("acorn.png", Texture.class);
}
```

They are all the textures we are going to use, so now we can start creating our textures.

Before we do I just want to introduce you to a class called `Sprite`. The `Sprite` class is an awesome class as it can not only hold our texture but also allows us to perform rotations and scaling on it. This will be needed as our acorns will roll along the ground and the building parts collapse and so on. So with that in mind, we are going to create our textures using this `Sprite` class.

For the creation of building parts and the enemies, I have created another class called `SpriteGenerator`. This class will inspect a body for user data and create a sprite that correctly corresponds to it.

The following is the code listing for the class:

```
public class SpriteGenerator {
  public static Sprite generateSpriteForBody(AssetManager
  assetManager, Body body) {
    if ("horizontal".equals(body.getUserData())) {
      return createSprite(assetManager, "obstacleHorizontal.png");
    }
    if ("vertical".equals(body.getUserData())) {
      return createSprite(assetManager, "obstacleVertical.png");
    }
    if ("enemy".equals(body.getUserData())) {
      return createSprite(assetManager, "bird.png");
    }
    return null;
  }
  private static Sprite createSprite(AssetManager assetManager,
  String textureName) {
    Sprite sprite = new Sprite(assetManager.get(textureName,
    Texture.class));
    sprite.setOrigin(sprite.getWidth() / 2, sprite.getHeight() /
    2);
    return sprite;
  }
}
```

As you can see, it only contains two methods, only one of which is the API. Hopefully, this should be straightforward for you to work out what is going on. Depending on the user data, we create a sprite with the texture that matches up. You will notice in the createSprite() method that we also set the origin; the reason for this is because the rotation ability of a sprite is based around that origin point. So, we simply set that to be the center of the texture.

Right, back to our GameScreen class, here we are now going to tie everything together. Firstly, let's define some new fields that we will be using for our textures:

```
private ObjectMap<Body, Sprite> sprites = new ObjectMap<>();;
private Sprite slingshot;
private Sprite squirrel;
private Sprite staticAcorn;
```

Firstly, we have a map that will provide us with the ability to look up sprites by the body that reflects them in the Box2D world. Then, we have three sprites that will be static parts of the game. The staticAcorn sprite, in case you are wondering, will be the acorn that sits in the slingshot and moves with the cursor before the acorn body is created and fired.

Now, we need to instantiate all these sprites and generate some sprites for the bodies. Let's update the show() method with the following additional code:

```
Array<Body> bodies = new Array<>();
world.getBodies(bodies);
for (Body body : bodies) {
  Sprite sprite = SpriteGenerator.generateSpriteForBody
  (nuttyGame.getAssetManager(), body);
  if (sprite != null) sprites.put(body, sprite);
}

slingshot = new Sprite(nuttyGame.getAssetManager().get
("slingshot.png", Texture.class));
slingshot.setPosition(170, 64);
squirrel = new Sprite(nuttyGame.getAssetManager().get
("squirrel.png", Texture.class));
squirrel.setPosition(32, 64);
staticAcorn = new Sprite(nuttyGame.getAssetManager().get
("acorn.png", Texture.class));
```

Here we have our SpriteGenerator class coming into play. We first of all query the world for all the bodies, and we then iterate over them and pass them and the AssetManager class to our generating class. If the body requires a sprite, it will be returned and we add it to the map.

I would like to say at this point that you could collect the bodies when you create them, but there is another way to do this, you could also create the sprite when you create the body and set it as its user data—that's fine too! The beauty of software development is that there isn't a right answer, there are usually several of them.

Finally, we create our static sprites and set their positions.

Before we run up this project and see where we are, we need to do just a couple more things.

Firstly, we are going to need a way to update the sprite positions every time the world is updated; otherwise they will never move!

So, we need to create a method called `updateSpritePositions()` and add it to our `GameScreen` class. Here it is:

```
private void updateSpritePositions() {
  for (Body body : sprites.keys()) {
    Sprite sprite = sprites.get(body);
    sprite.setPosition(
      convertMetresToUnits(body.getPosition().x) -
      sprite.getWidth() / 2f,
      convertMetresToUnits(body.getPosition().y) -
      sprite.getHeight() / 2f);
    sprite.setRotation(MathUtils.radiansToDegrees *
    body.getAngle());
  }
  staticAcorn.setPosition(firingPosition.x -
  staticAcorn.getWidth() / 2f, firingPosition.y -
  staticAcorn.getHeight() / 2f);
}
```

As you can see, it is fairly simple. We iterate over our map of bodies and sprites and update the sprite's position and rotation with that of the bodies. Finally, we update our static acorn to make the position of the firing position variable.

Now, we just add that to our `update()` method as follows:

```
private void update(float delta) {
  clearDeadBodies();
  world.step(delta, 6, 2);
  box2dCam.position.set(UNIT_WIDTH / 2, UNIT_HEIGHT / 2, 0);
  box2dCam.update();
  updateSpritePositions();
}
```

Finally, we should update our `clearDeadBodies()` method to remove the sprite that represents our enemy from the sprite map, so it will then disappear from view when the enemy is defeated:

```
private void clearDeadBodies() {
  for (Body body : toRemove) {
    sprites.remove(body);
    world.destroyBody(body);
  }
  toRemove.clear();
}
```

Next, we need to update our `createBullet()` method so that our acorn image is added to the map and will be rendered:

```
private void createBullet() {
  // Code ommitted for brevity
  Sprite sprite = new Sprite(nuttyGame.getAssetManager().get
  ("acorn.png", Texture.class));
  sprite.setOrigin(sprite.getWidth() / 2, sprite.getHeight() / 2);
  sprites.put(bullet, sprite);
  // Code ommitted for brevity
}
```

Ensure you place the following code above the `dispose()` call:

```
circleShape.dispose();
```

With the update cycle sorted and our acorns set to be rendered, we now need to update our `draw()` method so that everything is rendered correctly. Here is how the `draw()` method should look:

```
private void draw() {
  batch.setProjectionMatrix(camera.projection);
  batch.setTransformMatrix(camera.view);
  orthogonalTiledMapRenderer.render();
  batch.begin();
  for (Sprite sprite : sprites.values()) {
    sprite.draw(batch);
  }
  squirrel.draw(batch);
  staticAcorn.draw(batch);
  slingshot.draw(batch);
  batch.end();
}
```

Now, the absolute last thing to do! Comment out the `drawDebug()` call in our `render()` method so that we don't have the wire frames everywhere!

Ah but wait! Our sneaky artist has moved the location of the slingshot. We need to update our anchor position.

Let's use this as a test to see if you have been paying attention. See if you can work out what the position of the anchor should now be.

If you don't want to, here is what it should be set to now:

```
private final Vector2 anchor = new
Vector2(convertMetresToUnits(6.125f),
convertMetresToUnits(5.75f));
```

Ladies and gentleman – the main event!

Right, readers, this is the part we have all been waiting for. I know you have been itching to launch the game with the art and see it in all its glory. For those who have done that already, well done on being inquisitive to see the game in its various stages. For the rest, are you ready?

3...

2...

1...

Launch the project!

Yey, doesn't it look wonderful! How many shots do you have to fire before you defeat that naughty bird?

You should all be very proud of what you have just accomplished there. Whilst we don't have a score, menu screen, and a game state, you have already done these before in the previous games! Now is your chance to go back and take what we have and add it here. You now have all the tools to make a good-quality game with LibGDX.

Not only that, because of how we have made this game, you can go ahead and experiment with designing different levels in Tiled and see what works and doesn't.

I had a quick play with coming up with different ideas and playing with the strength of the acorn. So much fun making a game, don't you agree?

Summary

Well, what a chapter we had there! You managed to get your toes wet with Box2D and master it like a pro! Well, maybe not a pro just yet, however, you have the basis of a great game. There is a lot in Box2D we didn't cover, but hopefully this gives you a basic understanding and enough information to go forward and make other things with that fabulous engine. So, what did we do in this chapter? We looked at Box2D, how to use a brilliant tool like Tiled to make designing and building levels simple, used the Box2D debug rendering so that we could make our game before having the full art asset set, and had a look at a handy class called Sprite that helped us with rotation.

In the next chapter, we will introduce a handy technique that may be of some use to you going forward—object pooling! If we have a lot of objects that we could reuse rather than throw away and recreate, we should really look at pooling them, especially if they are expensive to create or our game is running in an environment where clean-up costs are high.

9
Even Angrier Birds!

Welcome to this chapter! I hope you enjoyed the previous chapter and are making your own games resembling Angry Birds. I also hope you used everything you learned in the previous chapters to really make it into a fully formed game.

In this chapter, we will cover a technique that will hopefully help you when you find yourself creating lots of instances of a certain type of object that are generally short-lived. We will look at object pooling and how LibGDX can provide the tools to help us use them. In this chapter, we'll take a look at the following topics:

* The how, what, and why of object pools
* Hey, look at all these acorns!

The how, what, and why of object pools

> *Object pooling is the principle of reusing inactive or "dead" objects, instead of creating new objects every time.*
>
> `-https://github.com/libgdx/libgdx/wiki/Memory-management#object-pooling`

I guess the best place to start is to talk about what an object pool is. An object pool is a pool of objects, bet you didn't see that coming, that can be reused after they become inactive. The pool can either be prefilled or filled on demand; hopefully, when you require one of these objects, there will be a "free" one available.

I suppose you are now wondering why you would want to do this. I suspect you are wondering, "Hey, I can just call "new" to create an object; perhaps it is an acorn sprite you are creating, and I can do this as much as I want and I don't see an impact." Perhaps, on the scale we are working on, you might get away with that. However, it isn't a mindset you should really adopt here. You have to remember that one of the wonderful things with LibGDX is that it is cross-platform with mobile devices. So, perhaps your game is going to go from running on your fabulous desktop/laptop development machine with your gigabytes of RAM and high-end graphics card to someone's three-year-old mobile smart phone that might have only megabytes of RAM available for your game and even less dedicated to video. So, first off, you might have "out of memory issues" where you create so many objects that the underlying OS might just call it quits on your game—not a good user experience!

The second issue that you might find is excessive slowing down of your game as, particularly on the Android platform, the garbage collector runs to clear out all the "inactive" objects that you created but no longer needed. This is where object pools can come into the picture and provide help. Imagine having to clear up hundreds of instances of an object type that has been created-on-the fly when, in fact, from a gameplay perspective only, say, three are in play at any point in time. If you had these objects in a pool, you would create the three required and then reuse them when you need to. Suddenly, all this excess processing that goes on for clearing up after your game goes away.

Object pools with LibGDX

Right, so hopefully you have an idea of what an object pool is and why an object pool can be useful. Let's look at how an object pool is created in LibGDX.

Before we dive into the code, I recommend that you refer to the wiki page on object pooling and memory management for LibGDX, which is available at the following URL:

```
https://github.com/libgdx/libgdx/wiki/Memory-management#object-pooling
```

I strongly suggest that you give it a browse as it will be an eye-opener on memory management.

So what does LibGDX offer to us game makers when it comes to creating object pools? Hopefully, those of you who checked out the preceding link already know the answer!

There are the three classes LibGDX provides:

- `Pool.Poolable`
- `Pool`
- `Pools`

The `Pool.Poolable` class is an interface that you implement on the object type class that you wish to be handled in a pool. Here is the interface in code:

```
static public interface Poolable {
   /** Resets the object for reuse. Object references should be
   nulled and fields may be set to default values. */
   public void reset ();
}
```

As you can see, it only has one method that you are required to provide an implementation to; that is the `reset()` method, which is required to clean up the object ready to be made available again in the pool. We will see more of this in the next section.

Next up is the `Pool` class; this is the pool itself. It contains the instantiations of the objects that we would like to pool. This class is typed, so we can only have all objects of the same type in there; otherwise, we will have all sorts of issues. This class is abstract, which means that we have to define our own class that extends this one. The reason for this is that we need to define how to create a new object for the pool; perhaps it requires some external input such as a reference to a texture that is used for the visual representation. There are two parameters that are required to construct the pool and they are the maximum number of objects in the pool and the initial capacity. It should be noted now that the maximum number is a soft limit. If you request an object and there are none free, a new one will be created. However, when it comes to returning the objects to the pool, if the pool is full, they will be reset but not added back to the pool. I would also like to highlight that the initial capacity doesn't prefill the pool for you; all it does is help to set up the backing array. This is a good thing as, then, you won't get slight pauses in your game should the backing array wish to grow.

To take an object from the pool, there is a method called `obtain()` that returns either a fresh instance or one from the pool.

When it comes to the time that the game no longer uses this object, as it may have gone out of play, then call the `free()` method on the pool with the object to be returned.

Just before we move on to the final class that LibGDX has to offer, I want to take this opportunity to highlight the caveat that is mentioned on the LibGDX wiki. It is possible to leak objects from the pool; just because it is returned to the pool doesn't mean other objects do not automatically clear their references to that returned object. This means you will see some odd behavior in your game if you are not careful.

Finally, we have the `Pools` class. This class, as you can imagine, contains all the pool instances that are provided to it, allowing you to have static access to them anywhere in your code. For the sake of what I would like to cover in this chapter, we will not be using this class. I just wanted you to be aware that this class exists, for when you start having lots of pools.

Hey, look at all these acorns!

Now we have a handle on what an object pool is, why we need one, and how we can use LibGDX to look after one for us. Next, we need to look at how we can use one in Nutty Birds.

I am going to take a liberty with the gameplay and make a fundamental change to the way the game is played. We will design the game in such a way that we can only have three acorns on the screen at on time. Whenever you fire another while three are already in play, the oldest will be removed from the game. This may sound rather crude, but our aim here is to try out an object pool. Once we are done, you can try and shape the game the way you wish to.

Pooling the acorns

Our first task is to move our acorn from a `Sprite` instance to a class in its own right. This class will implement the `Pool.Poolable` interface.

The following is the code listing for our new `Acorn` class:

```
public class Acorn implements Pool.Poolable {
  private final Sprite sprite;
  public Acorn(AssetManager assetManager) {
    sprite = new Sprite(assetManager.get("acorn.png",
    Texture.class));
    sprite.setOrigin(sprite.getWidth() / 2, sprite.getHeight() /
    2);
  }

  public void setPosition(float x, float y) {
```

```
      sprite.setPosition(x, y);
   }

   public void setRotation(float degrees) {
      sprite.setRotation(degrees);
   }

   public float getWidth() {
      return sprite.getWidth();
   }

   public float getHeight() {
      return sprite.getHeight();
   }

   public void draw(Batch batch) {
      sprite.draw(batch);
   }

   @Override
   public void reset() {
      sprite.setPosition(0,0);
      sprite.setRotation(0F);
   }
}
```

As you can see, our new class contains the `Sprite` class that we originally created in the `GameScreen` class; it implements the `Pool.Poolable` interface and we delegate four methods from the `Sprite` class. We implement the `reset()` method as required, and in return we reset all the rotation and the position back to zero. In our constructor, we pass in our `AssetManager` instance so we can get access to our texture.

This class is now ready to go and be part of an object pool!

Our next step is to create our own acorn pool. To do this, we need to create a class that extends the `Pool` class. Let's create a class called `AcornPool` and extend that `Pool` class.

Here is the code you we will end up with:

```
public class AcornPool extends Pool<Acorn> {
  public static final int ACORN_COUNT = 3;
  private final AssetManager assetManager;
  public AcornPool(AssetManager assetManager) {
    super(ACORN_COUNT,ACORN_COUNT);
    this.assetManager = assetManager;
  }

  @Override
  protected Acorn newObject() {
    return new Acorn(assetManager);
  }
}
```

As you can see, we have typed our Pool class to be that of the Acorn class. We pass in our AssetManager instance, as we will need this later on. We have also defined our parameters for the pool with the ACORN_COUNT constant. Finally, we implement our newObject() method. Here, we just return a freshly created Acorn instance.

The next task is a rather big one: we need to update the GameScreen class to use this new pool.

First, we should define our new pool class as a variable but also have a separate map for managing our bodies to the Acorn instances. Add the following code to the GameScreen class:

```
private AcornPool acornPool;
private OrderedMap<Body, Acorn> acorns = new OrderedMap<>();
```

Now, in the show() method, we will instantiate the pool as follows:

```
acornPool = new AcornPool(nuttyGame.getAssetManager());
```

Perfect! Next, we need to update the createAcorn() method, which was previously called createBullet(), but I have renamed it since we now know what the projectile turned out to be. We need to change the way we create the acorn, from instantiation to using the pool. Let's take a look at the following code snippet:

```
private void createAcorn() {
  CircleShape circleShape = new CircleShape();
  circleShape.setRadius(0.5f);
  BodyDef bd = new BodyDef();
  bd.type = BodyDef.BodyType.DynamicBody;
  Body acorn = world.createBody(bd);
  acorn.setUserData("acorn");
```

```
    acorn.createFixture(circleShape, 1);
    acorn.setTransform(new
    Vector2(convertUnitsToMetres(firingPosition.x),
    convertUnitsToMetres(firingPosition.y)), 0);
    acorns.put(acorn, acornPool.obtain());
    circleShape.dispose();
    float velX = Math.abs((MAX_STRENGTH * -MathUtils.cos(angle) *
    (distance / 100f)));
    float velY = Math.abs((MAX_STRENGTH * -MathUtils.sin(angle) *
    (distance / 100f)));
    acorn.setLinearVelocity(velX, velY);
}
```

This is how the method should look. As you can see, we have replaced the creation code with a simple call to the pool to obtain our instance. At this point, we don't know if it is fresh or reused. However, if we do this correctly, we won't care or notice!

Finally, we need to update our code so we are referencing the new acorn map, instead of the previous sprite map. Let's take a look at the following code snippet:

```
private void updateAcornPositions() {
  for (Body body : acorns.keySet()) {
    Acorn acorn = acorns.get(body);
    acorn.setPosition(convertMetresToUnits(body.getPosition().x) -
    acorn.getWidth() / 2f,
    convertMetresToUnits(body.getPosition().y) - acorn.getHeight()
    / 2f);
    acorn.setRotation(MathUtils.radiansToDegrees *
    body.getAngle());
  }
}
```

Here I created a new method to take care of the updates! We now need to add a call to this method in our `update()` method.

Next, we need to update our `draw()` method to draw from our new acorn map, as follows:

```
private void draw() {
  // Code omitted for brevity
  for (Acorn acorn : acorns.values()) {
    acorn.draw(batch);
  }
  // Code omitted for brevity
}
```

Brilliant! If you run the project now, it'll look and behave like it did earlier. However, we are not limiting our acorns yet and, if you look at our pool in a debug view, you will see that we are doing nothing but just creating new instances.

Freeing the acorns!

We need to apply our limit to the acorns and ensure that they are returned to the pool. This is actually a straightforward step.

We need to check the map size; if it is at our maximum, which in this case is 3, we take the first entry offered by the map. Next, we can queue up to have the Box2D body removed from the world, remove the acorn from the map, and then return the acorn to the pool. We should create a method called `checkLimitAndRemoveAcornIfNecessary()` and place it in our `GameScreen` class. The following is the code required to do this:

```
private void checkLimitAndRemoveAcornIfNecessary() {
  if (acorns.size == AcornPool.ACORN_COUNT) {
    Body body = acorns.keys().iterator().next();
    toRemove.add(body);
    Acorn acorn = acorns.remove(body);
    acornPool.free(acorn);
  }
}
```

As you can see, we check the map. We grab the first offered instance, and queue it up to be removed. Next, we remove the map entry and return it to the pool. To make it perform a bit more than expected, we can change our map from an `ObjectMap` instance to an `OrderedMap` instance as this will keep track of the insertions made in the map. Let's take a look at the following code:

```
private OrderedMap<Body, Acorn> acorns = new OrderedMap<>();
```

Our final step is to add the call to the preceding method in our `createAcorn()` method just before we obtain an acorn from the pool:

```
checkLimitAndRemoveAcornIfNecessary();
acorns.put(acorn, acornPool.obtain());
```

If we run up the project now, you will find that we are now limited to three acorns. Believe it or not, the sprites being used are all the same instance. If you don't believe me as a trace out on the `newObject()` method of the `AcornPool` class and see how many get created.

Summary

Well, that wraps up Nutty Birds. In this chapter, we looked at object pools and how you can use one to reduce the need to create new objects all the time. We also took time to understand the need for this and the impact that it can have on performance. This is not to say that an object pool is the right answer every time — it isn't. It is a useful tool you now have in your game-making toolbox; the trick is to learn when to use it and when not. Unfortunately, I can't answer this with a straight answer; it really comes down to the game you make and the game mechanics you implement.

Coming up in the next chapter, we move away from making games to look at how to use LibGDX to deliver your game onto different platforms, such as Android, iOS, and HTML5. I look forward to seeing you there!

10
Exporting Our Games to the Platforms

Welcome! In this chapter, we are going to move away from making games. I know, I know, I enjoyed myself too and we made some great stuff! But you see, LibGDX is so much more than what we were using it for till this point. In this chapter, we are going to look at the crossplatform features LibGDX has. In fact, this is probably what encouraged you to use LibGDX in the first place. Imagine, writing your game once and then being able to export it to Android, iOS, HTML, Desktop, and others. Well, this is what this chapter is going to be all about. The following are the topics that we will cover in this chapter:

- Using all the platforms
- Looking closer – Android
- Looking closer – iOS
- Looking closer – HTML

Using all the platforms

Hopefully by now, you are well on your way to being able to make your own games. We have been through all the main areas of LibGDX that you will likely use, and we also showed you other things LibGDX can do that you can take further with you.

But now, you are ready! Ready to take your game to the world. Except, you didn't come here to just make a game for desktop. You came here because you wanted your game to run on Android, iOS, and maybe even a browser version.

Am I correct in thinking that?

Of course I am!

To start off with, we are going to revisit our friendly setup tool that we have used throughout this book. But this time, we are going to have all the boxes ticked for subprojects! That's right, all the boxes! Let's take a look at the following steps:

1. So, let's launch the setup tool once again. You should be getting quite good at filling in the first part by now.

2. Make sure your **Sub Projects** pane looks like this:

3. Then, untick all the extensions, as we won't be doing anything fancy here.

4. Finally, click on **Generate** and import your project into your favorite IDE!

If you want to read more on how to utilize multiple environments, I suggest you to go through the LibGDX wiki for more information. Particularly, visit
`https://github.com/libgdx/libgdx/wiki/Gradle-on-the-Commandline`.

Looking closer – Android

First up, we will look at Android as a platform to publish the package to, and deploy the package.

Upon opening the project that we just set up, you will notice a few differences from what we had before. Note that there are many more useful directories and we now have one directory for Android, HTML, and iOS. If you open up the core directory, you will see that the asset directory has disappeared, it is now in the Android directory. Your structure should look similar to the following:

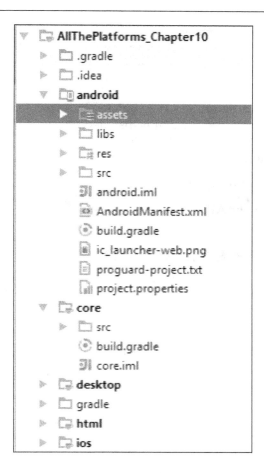

Thanks to the setup tool, a lot has been preconfigured for us. So much so that we can launch the Android simulator with just one command line. However, before we do that, I suggest that you run the desktop version first just to confirm that we have the default "Hello World" application working.

Did that work for you? Excellent!

Now, we should try running the simulator. Personally, I rarely use the simulator, I much prefer loading it onto a real device. I just want to show you that this is possible, though, in case you don't have access to a device or you wish to try different screen sizes. I should point out that the simulator's speed does depend largely on your development computer.

There are two ways to launch the simulator. Either we can launch it from the command line or we can launch it straight from the IDE. I will try to show you both; however, I am using Android Studio/IntelliJ, so the process might be different if you are using Eclipse.

Before we launch the simulator, let's very quickly build a debug version of our APK — an APK is the generated file that is installed on an Android device. To do that, you can use the IDE or the command line to generate the APK file. In your project folder, run the following.

```
gradlew android:assembleDebug
```

This will then generate our APK.

Launching the emulator from an IDE

I hope you are ready for the long and really complex process that this involves.

Only kidding!

When you imported the project, Android Studio/IntelliJ was clever enough to pick up on the fact that there is an Android project there and provided you with a run configuration. In fact, it should be selected as default so you can just hit the run button.

The run button is the green arrow next to the Android configuration.

Next, you will be presented with the Choose Device dialog.

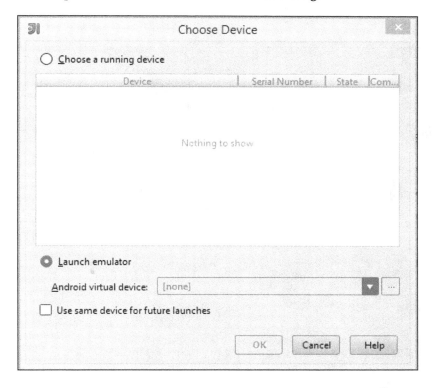

As you can see, we will need to set up a virtual device. If you click on the button to the right, it will launch the Android Virtual Device Manager; from here, we can create one project.

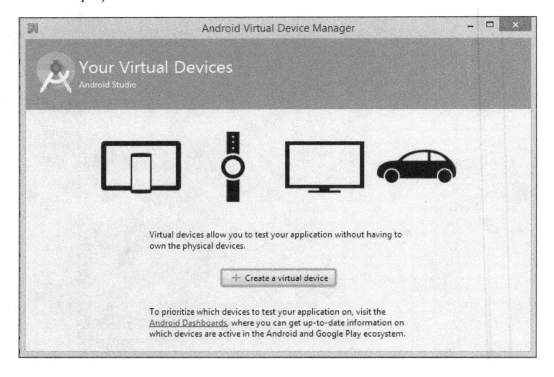

Let's take a look at the following steps:

1. If you click on **Create a virtual device**, you will be presented with a plethora of different hardware types and device profiles.

2. Since we are here to focus on mobile phones, let's just select **Phone** and then **Nexus 4**.

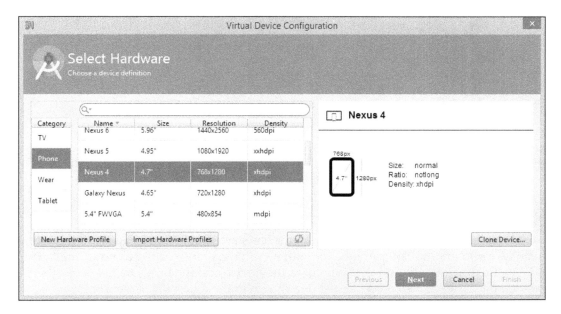

To be honest, you could pick whichever hardware profile you like. However, for the sake of this book, I will be using Nexus 4.

3. Once you click on **Next**, you will be prompted to pick a system image. For now, just pick **armeabi-v7a**. I currently have API Level 22 installed so I am choosing the same.

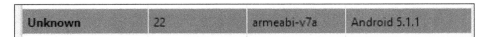

4. Finally, you will be presented with a configuration panel; for now, you can leave the configuration as it is. Later, you can revisit this and play around with the different settings. Click on **Finish** to complete the setup.

We will now add an entry in our Virtual Devices. If we exit and return to our **Choose Device** dialog screen, we can now pick our chosen virtual device.

Excellent! Hit **Run** and let the computer take care of the rest!

While this is loading up, there are tools available that will help make the emulator run faster. One of them is the Intel Hardware Accelerated Execution Manager. I didn't cover how to use this as it requires your computer to have an Intel CPU with Virtualization technology; if your development computer does, perfect—you can get it set up from `http://developer.android.com/tools/devices/emulator.html#acceleration`.

In the meantime, let's hope that the emulator has started up; it has? Excellent! It looks just like a real phone! You can interact with it with the mouse acting as your finger. If you swipe up, you will find that it unlocks the device and the LibGDX test project will be seen on the screen. It looks like the one shown in the following screenshot:

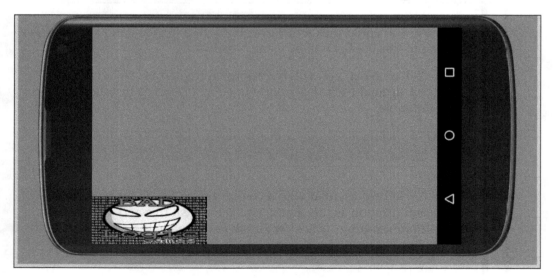

Now, we will do the same, but from the command line.

Launching the emulator from the command line

This is going to be very similar to the IDE approach; however, we will need to tell the emulator to install our APK first.

First up, we can run the Android Virtual Device Manager by entering the following in the command line:

```
android avd
```

We will be presented with a different dialog from the one in the IDE; this was wrapped it in a nicer UI for us.

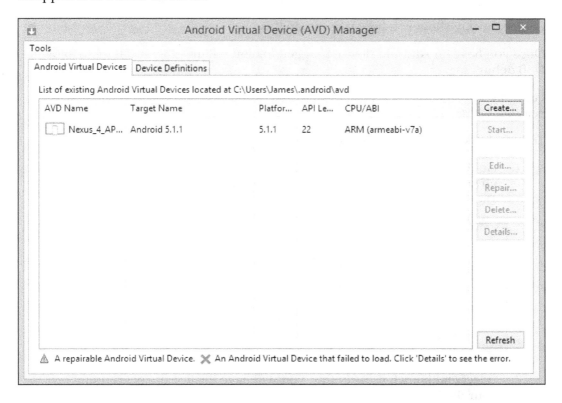

As you can see, it is different, but I ensure you that all the options are the same. If you don't have an entry, you can try the Create process. It is a simplistic version of the one that we had before.

Once you have done that, we can launch our virtual device. Select it and click on **Start**.

While the device is booting up, let's get ready to upload our APK to the device. Navigate your way to the project folder and when the device has loaded, run the following command:

```
adb install android\build\outputs\apk\android-debug.apk
```

You will then find the game in the menu of the Virtual Android Device. Navigate your way there and you will find it.

Perfect! You can now run your game in an emulator. As I said previously, I much prefer running the game on a real device because not only is the performance better, but it also gives you a much better impression of how the game is going to perform.

Let me quickly show you how you can do this.

Once you have an Android device plugged in, you will need your device to allow USB debugging.

For more information regarding this process, visit `http://developer.android.com/tools/device.html`.

To launch the project from the IDE, perform the following steps:

1. Go through the same process as before. Except, instead of launching the virtual device, we are going to select your device should be in the **Choose Device** dialog. Let's take a look at the following screenshot:

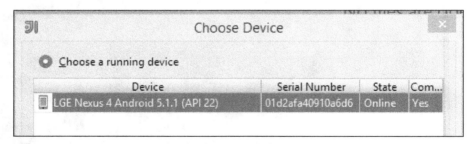

2. Select and launch it. After this, you will have the test project running on your device!

3. To do this from the command line, simply run this command in your project directory:

```
gradlew android:installDebug android:run
```

As a side note, you may find that the command line fails on occasion if it hasn't successfully uninstalled the application, as it will think you are trying to install the same application that is already there.

There you go, you are now able to launch your game on a device.

Hang on, how does it work?

Ah, you caught me! We jumped straight to seeing something working without discussing how all of it works. Well essentially, your Android subproject can be seen as similar to the Desktop subproject, both have the core subproject as a dependency and both create an instance of your game. Check out the `AndroidLauncher` class and the `DesktopLauncher` class and you will see the similarities.

I am not going to cover how Android works here as that is beyond the scope of what this book is about. There are plenty of resources out there if you wish to know more. I recommend that you start from the Android website: `http://developer.android.com`.

Release the Kraken!

Alright, maybe not the Kraken, but at some point, you will need to generate a release APK that you will want to upload to certain online stores where you can make it available for the world to download and play.

I won't be covering the app store part, but I will show you how to make sure your APK is signed and uses something called ProGuard to reduce and obfuscate your code.

Firstly, let's cover signing. Why does your APK needs to be signed and what does this mean? Well, Android requires you to sign your release APK with a certificate to identify you as the author of the app. It is fairly common for you to use a self-signed certificate.

When it comes to generating your own certificate, refer to `http://developer.android.com/tools/publishing/app-signing.html` on how to create your own certificate.

To have the APK signed as part of the build process, we need to update the `build.gradle` file in the Android subproject, as this doesn't get generated for us. Let's take a look at the following steps:

1. In the file, update the Android module, as follows:

```
signingConfigs {
  release {
    storeFile file(RELEASE_STORE_FILE)
    storePassword RELEASE_STORE_PASSWORD
    keyAlias RELEASE_KEY_ALIAS
    keyPassword RELEASE_KEY_PASSWORD
  }
}
```

   Here, the text in caps will need to be replaced with your information. I highly recommend you to not keep your passwords in this file, but instead have them in the `gradle.properties` file in the `.gradle` directory in your home location and then reference them, like we did previously.

2. However, this isn't the end of it, we need to now run Proguard. The reason for doing this is that it will reduce the overall size of your APK as well making it very hard to reverse-engineer your game should someone choose to do so. Luckily for us, LibGDX generates a base for Proguard. In fact, now is a good time if you are interested to visit their website: http://proguard.sourceforge.net/.

3. To utilize the code in our build, we need to add `buildTypes` to our Android module and specify the following:

```
buildTypes {
  release {
    signingConfig signingConfigs.release
    minifyEnabled true
    proguardFile getDefaultProguardFile('proguard-android-
    optimize.txt')
    proguardFile 'proguard-project.txt'
  }
}
```

   Here we are saying that, when performing a release build, we need to sign using our signing configuration and enable minify, which will handle the Proguard execution.

4. Finally, to perform the release, run the following command in the project directory:

```
gradlew android:assembleRelease
```

You will then find a release APK in the outputs directory.

There you have it. Now you should now be able to release your game on Android!

Looking closer – iOS

Ah iOS! The platform that transformed mobile app development and brought it to the mainstream. Hey! You are probably wondering that LibGDX is a Java-based framework, so how on earth does it run on iOS? Apple banned Java Runtimes long ago. Well you are correct, the game isn't exported as you might think it is. In fact, an additional tool called RoboVM is used. RoboVM's project aim was to allow Java developers to develop the game on the iOS platform, and the best bit is that the game will have a native-style performance. It doesn't need a runtime to launch. How is this possible? Well, RoboVM compiles the bytecode, generated by the Java compiler, with machine code.

To check out RoboVM, visit its website, http://robovm.com/.

LibGDX and RoboVM have what seems to be a tight partnership and work extremely well together. In fact, out-of-the-box – the project set up tool – you can build applications for iOS with RoboVM.

I would like you to note now that like we did for Android, I am not going to cover how to set up an Apple Developer account or create provisioning profiles, key chains, and so on. There are plenty of documentation available on this topic.

Check out Apple's developer site https://developer.apple.com/ for more information,

As before, like Android, you can see that we have an iOS submodule and it contains the configuration required to create an IPA – an IPA is equivalent to Android's APK. For development, you can dive straight in. For releases, it is a bit more involved in the game. To release the game, you will need to be on a Mac – I use a Mac Mini and solely for release purposes. You will need Xcode installed – this is available from the App Store on the Mac, a developer account, and Xcode signed in with that account.

If you look at the iOS submodule, you will see an IOSLauncher class. When you look, you will see some familiar code, essentially, the platform configuration and an instantiation of our game.

To build a debug IPA, you can use the command line and run the following:

```
gradlew ios:createIPA
```

However, this isn't of much use to us; you can launch the simulator, as follows:

```
gradlew ios:launchIPhoneSimulator
gradlew ios:launchIPadSimulator
```

If you have a device connected to a Mac, use the following:

```
gradlew ios:launchIOSDevice
```

This is really about it for iOS. It is that straightforward. Thanks to the use of a developer account and Apple's xcode application, everything was automatically signed and verified for us.

For more information on how to distribute your game on iOS, I recommend you to visit https://developer.apple.com/library/ios/documentation/IDEs/ Conceptual/AppDistributionGuide/Introduction/Introduction.html.

Looking closer – HTML

The last platform we are going to look at is HTML. This might perplex you even more than iOS did. How on earth do we go from Java to HTML! Luckily, Google has the answer—**Google Web Toolkit** (**GWT**). By using GWT will convert Java classes into a JavaScript equivalent.

However, there are some limitations with the HTML export. I would like to add that HTML exports are getting smaller with each release and the smaller releases are the support for certain Java classes. You might find sometimes that there isn't a JavaScript equivalent available and GWT will refuse to compile the code. But having said that, I have used it a lot before and there are always ways around this, and LibGDX has full GWT support from the onset. So as long as you don't stray too far from LibGDX, you will be able to create an HTML game!

Check out the GWT website, http://www.gwtproject.org/, for more information.

Getting ready to launch

Like with the other plaforms, HTML has it's own submodule and a `HtmlLauncher` class, in which you can see a platform-specific configuration object and the game being created. Very, very simple!

You will notice that there are also *.gwt.xml files here and in the core submodule, these are used so that GWT can find the original source of the code to be translated.

To get the game up-and-running with HTML, on the command line run the following command:

```
gradlew html:superDev
```

Once it is run, you will find that it hasn't exited, but instead, it has run its own webserver to provide us the HTML file and JavaScript to us.

Excellent, now if you visit that website in your browser, you will be presented with instructions on how you can enable the dev mode—making debugging easier. Once you have loaded that page, you can go to http://localhost:8080/html/.

The game will then be loaded.

Excellent!

Finally, I want to cover releasing of the game, as you won't want people playing your game in your browser!

Run the following command:

```
gradlew html:dist
```

Everything you need to upload on your website will be in the `html/build/dist` directory. It is as simple as that!

Summary

Well, I hope that you have an understanding of what it takes to package up and deploy your game on multiple platforms, and in fact, considering how Gradle works, it is entirely possible to build everything you need in one go:

```
gradlew android:assembleRelease ios:createIPA html:dist
```

I know because I have done this!

In this chapter, we looked at how to set up our Android releases and how to export the project with iOS, and we then looked at HTML and how we can generate JavaScript to cover this platform.

In the next chapter, we are going to look at how to integrate a third-party service and how to interact with it in LibGDX.

11
Third-party Services

Well, we have made it. This is the last chapter of this book. I know, I am sad too, but after this chapter, I hope I leave you with a sense of accomplishment and enough knowledge that you can go off on your own and start making games in LibGDX.

Before you go, I would like to cover one last thing and that is how to integrate your game with third-party services. For example, there are social media platforms out there that have game-based integration. Whether it is achievements or leader boards that you are after, they will have them. In this chapter, we are going to look at how to integrate the game with a fictitious social media platform that provides high scores. This fictitious platform, which we will call as FriendFace, provides an Android library and we will use this in our integration. We will cover the following topics in this chapter:

- How to use platform-dependent libraries
- Keeping the game cross-platform-friendly

How to use platform-dependent libraries

In your quest to integrate third-party services, you will find that the providers very often do not provide you with similar-level tools to use their platform. For example, a user may have a library on a Maven repository somewhere and all you have to do is add the Gradle reference and Gradle will do the rest. Other users might have a Gradle-enabled project that you need to download and add to your project manually or just a simple JAR file that you need to download and add, and nothing else. We will quickly cover how you can go about importing the dependency into your project.

Now, the thing to bear in mind here is that, if you are using an Android library, then the project needs to solely exist on the Android subproject. The core project knows nothing about Android and has no idea about any of the Android classes that may be required to compile your project once you add the reference.

The nice way – via Maven

If the third-party you are interested in using has its library Mavenised – it is in a public access Maven repository – then all we have to do is edit our `build.gradle` build, for the whole project, and add an entry.

So, if we carry on with the use of an Android library as an example, we need to update the Android subproject entry as:

```
project(":android") {
  apply plugin: "android"
  configurations { natives }
  dependencies {
    compile project(":core")
    compile "com.badlogicgames.gdx:gdx-backend-
    android:$gdxVersion"
    compile 'com.madeup.friendface:friendface-android-sdk:1.0.0'
    natives "com.badlogicgames.gdx:gdx-
    platform:$gdxVersion:natives-armeabi"
    natives "com.badlogicgames.gdx:gdx-
    platform:$gdxVersion:natives-armeabi-v7a"
    natives "com.badlogicgames.gdx:gdx-
    platform:$gdxVersion:natives-x86"
  }
}
```

As you can see, adding the dependency to the project is just one simple line:

```
compile 'com.madeup.friendface:friendface-android-sdk:1.0.0'
```

When you run the program, bear in mind that this is fake and doesn't exist – this is for when you have a real-life dependency. At that time, Gradle will go off and resolve it for you and download the library, which will be add to the projects classpath. Then, if FriendFace releases a new version, we just change the build number at the end of the program and it will get updated.

Pretty nifty I think!

An alternative to Maven – A project/JAR file

OK, so the next third-party provider isn't as helpful, to us at least. For this, you have to visit their website and discover that they have a ZIP file that you need to download. This archive contains a Gradle project that you need to place into yours. Generally, I place these inside a directory in the subproject that it belongs to. Next, I update the `settings.gradle` file of the main project to include this. Say the file is in the Android subproject, I have the following:

```
include 'desktop', 'android', 'core'
include ':android:libs:thirdparty'
```

You will then need to reference it in a similar way to what we did for the Maven dependency:

```
compile project(":android:libs:thirdparty")
```

However, there are downsides to this approach. Firstly, you now have enlarged the size of your project; if you work in a team, this project is now very much tied to your code base. Secondly, it is not as easy as the Maven dependency when it comes to updating the library. Finally, back in the team scenario, if you don't package this with your project and ask other team members to download it, they might download the wrong version and cause inconsistencies with your code base.

Adding just a JAR file in Gradle is actually really simple. You could create a directory, I call it "libs", in your subproject and place your JAR file there. Then, in the Gradle build file, use the following line in your dependencies:

```
compile fileTree(dir: 'libs', include: ['*.jar'])
```

This line is actually a catchall. Any JAR files in this directory will get picked up, which is generally what you would want anyway.

Keeping it cross-platform friendly

I hope you have managed to keep up with where we are at the moment with the third-party libraries. This sounds a little daunting at first, but once you have done it a couple of times, you will see that it is pretty straightforward.

What we are going to look at now is how you would interact with one of these libraries if you were to use one.

FriendFace for Android

Carrying on with our made-up social network called FriendFace, we are going to implement the social network's Android integration that it has. It doesn't offer anything fancy other than the ability for us to post a player's name and score. Then, FriendFace does whatever it is that it does with the name and score; perhaps it shows it to the player's friends?

The following is how we are going to define the `FriendFaceAPI` class:

```
public class FriendFaceAPI {
  public void postScore(String name, int score) {
    //Some code, the library may be opensource or not - who knows!
  }
}
```

Pretty straight forward!

FriendFace's Android integration comes in the form of a Gradle-based Android library project. This means that we will have to add it to our Android subproject.

I have already created a project that includes all this—refer to the code provided in this chapter.

Once you have imported it in your IDE, if you look inside the Android subproject, you will see a `libs` directory that contains the `FriendFace` library project!

Now, what will we do? For the sake of simplicity, we will use the default project and submit a score every time the space bar is pressed.

Hang on! I bet you are thinking that the game code is in the Core subproject and FriendFace only offers the capability available in the Android subproject; how on earth am I going to bridge that gap?

Well, you would be correct in thinking that. We can't have the `FriendFace` library in the Core subproject; for example, what will happen when we try to run it on iOS? So, what we need to do is create an interface and implementation-style approach.

In our Core subproject, we will create an interface class that we will call as `ScoreHandler` and it will have the following code:

```
public interface ScoreHandler {
  void postScore(String name, int score);
}
```

Looks familiar? Well it should, as it has the same API as FriendFace. I should point out that we can get away with this for now as the API is quite simplistic; however, as you integrate more complex third-party services across your different platforms, it may not be as easy to unify this API with the social network.

Next, we are going to update the game class; in my case, it is just called as the MyGdxGame class so that it refers to this new interface. The class ends up looking like this:

```
public class MyGdxGame extends ApplicationAdapter {
    SpriteBatch batch;
    Texture img;
    ScoreHandler scoreHandler;

    @Override
    public void create() {
        batch = new SpriteBatch();
        img = new Texture("badlogic.jpg");
    }

    @Override
    public void render() {
        if (Gdx.input.isKeyPressed(Input.Keys.SPACE)) {
            scoreHandler.postScore("James", 1000);
        }

        Gdx.gl.glClearColor(1, 0, 0, 1);
        Gdx.gl.glClear(GL20.GL_COLOR_BUFFER_BIT);
        batch.begin();
        batch.draw(img, 0, 0);
        batch.end();
    }
}
```

So, as we said before, on the tap of a space bar, we will call the method. The quick thinkers among you will probably be screaming at the book saying "There is going to be a NullPointerException exception!" and you are quite right—however, we are not done yet!

We need to provide an Android implementation of our interface; we can do this by creating a class in our Android subproject called `ScoreHandlerAndroid`, and it will implement our `ScoreHandler` interface class as:

```
public class ScoreHandlerAndroid implements ScoreHandler {
  @Override
  public void postScore(String name, int score) {

  }
}
```

Right now, this code doesn't do anything—however, as it is in the Android subproject, where the `FriendFaceAPI` class is, we can delegate the method call to a reference of it!

Now, our class becomes like this:

```
public class ScoreHandlerAndroid implements ScoreHandler {
  private final FriendFaceAPI friendFaceAPI;
  public ScoreHandlerAndroid(FriendFaceAPI friendFaceAPI) {
    this.friendFaceAPI = friendFaceAPI;
  }

  @Override
  public void postScore(String name, int score) {
    friendFaceAPI.postScore(name, score);
  }
}
```

Excellent! Now, we pass in our reference and then delegate the call. Next, we need to create this reference in our `AndroidLauncher` class:

```
public class AndroidLauncher extends AndroidApplication {
  @Override
  protected void onCreate (Bundle savedInstanceState) {
    super.onCreate(savedInstanceState);
    FriendFaceAPI friendFaceAPI = new FriendFaceAPI();
    ScoreHandlerAndroid scoreHandlerAndroid = new
    ScoreHandlerAndroid(friendFaceAPI);
    AndroidApplicationConfiguration config = new
    AndroidApplicationConfiguration();
    initialize(new MyGdxGame(scoreHandlerAndroid), config);
  }
}
```

Finally, we just need to update the game class again to get a constructor that accepts a `ScoreHandler` reference and sets the local variable. Here is the snippet to do so from the updated class:

```
ScoreHandler scoreHandler;

public MyGdxGame(ScoreHandler scoreHandler) {
  this.scoreHandler = scoreHandler;
}
```

There you have it. Now, you can access the FriendFace API and post a score.

What you will find is that, after setting a constructor on the game class, you need to go around and update the reference on all platforms, such as desktop, for example. Here, you may want to create a dummy implementation for each platform. How the dummy will function is really based on what you, and the game, are expecting to happen from the integration. Of course, you may have a desktop library for FriendFace. If you wish to implement it, it's excellent; add that library to the project and create another implementation. Simple!

A potential trap! (Android)

OK, imagine that you want to a create a few games now. You are fairly confident about how LibGDX works and you are going to integrate more third-party services — perhaps you want to add an advertisement to your game, which is not an uncommon scenario if you want to make a little bit of revenue from it.

You select your advertisement platform that you wish to use and add their library to your project. You start creating interfaces and implementations and run your game on Android. Then, you get to the point where you expect an advertisement to pop up and, all of a sudden, it crashes. You may be thinking that this is a bit odd. You check your code and double-check the documentation for Android that the third-party offers, but find that they are all the same and correct. You finally come back to this book and you are now reading these words. What you saw now is an error when two worlds collide; chances are that your advertising platform is required to run on an Android UI thread. However, the calls you are making come from the game thread — the OpenGL-enabled LibGDX thread — and Android is upset because you are calling the code from the wrong thread!

To fix this, we can use an object called `Handler`. This class allows us to send messages between the threads. When we create a `Handler`, we can specify a `handleMessage()` method that we can use to handle these messages. So, we may want something like this in our `AndroidLauncher` class:

```
private final Handler handler = new Handler() {
  @Override
  public void handleMessage(Message message) {
    if (message.what == 1) ad.show();
  }
};
```

Next, we just need a way to send a message. This is pretty straightforward as the `Handler` class has lots of useful methods; one which we will use is to call `sendEmptyMessage()`. So in our code, where we toggle for our advertisement, we can have the following code:

```
public void displayAdvert() {
  handler.sendEmptyMessage(1);
}
```

It is that easy! Of course, there are many complex things we can do, but I just wanted to highlight this scenario, as I have tripped over such a situation many times before.

Summary

In this chapter, we looked at how to integrate third-party services with our game; we saw the different ways a third-party provider can present their library to us, and how we can integrate it in our game. We then took as an example a fictitious third-party provider so we could learn how to interact with that library from our core game code. Finally, we covered a little trick that seems to catch people out a lot, me included!

Coming up, in the next chapter... Oh, there isn't another one...

That's it, readers, we have made it to the end of this book. I hope you enjoyed making these games, I know I have. You learned the basics with Sammy the snake and made UI components with the Flappy bee before we looked at the more advanced features of LibGDX with Pete the squirrel and his funky world of physics.

I look forward to playing your games on my Desktop/Android/iOS device in the future!

Index

A

B

C

Thank you for buying
LibGDX Game Development By Example

About Packt Publishing

Packt, pronounced 'packed', published its first book, *Mastering phpMyAdmin for Effective MySQL Management*, in April 2004, and subsequently continued to specialize in publishing highly focused books on specific technologies and solutions.

Our books and publications share the experiences of your fellow IT professionals in adapting and customizing today's systems, applications, and frameworks. Our solution-based books give you the knowledge and power to customize the software and technologies you're using to get the job done. Packt books are more specific and less general than the IT books you have seen in the past. Our unique business model allows us to bring you more focused information, giving you more of what you need to know, and less of what you don't.

Packt is a modern yet unique publishing company that focuses on producing quality, cutting-edge books for communities of developers, administrators, and newbies alike. For more information, please visit our website at www.packtpub.com.

About Packt Open Source

In 2010, Packt launched two new brands, Packt Open Source and Packt Enterprise, in order to continue its focus on specialization. This book is part of the Packt Open Source brand, home to books published on software built around open source licenses, and offering information to anybody from advanced developers to budding web designers. The Open Source brand also runs Packt's Open Source Royalty Scheme, by which Packt gives a royalty to each open source project about whose software a book is sold.

Writing for Packt

We welcome all inquiries from people who are interested in authoring. Book proposals should be sent to author@packtpub.com. If your book idea is still at an early stage and you would like to discuss it first before writing a formal book proposal, then please contact us; one of our commissioning editors will get in touch with you.

We're not just looking for published authors; if you have strong technical skills but no writing experience, our experienced editors can help you develop a writing career, or simply get some additional reward for your expertise.

Learning LibGDX Game Development
Second Edition

ISBN: 978-1-78355-477-5   Paperback: 478 pages

Wield the power of the LibGDX framework to create a cross-platform game

1. Write your game code once and run it on a multitude of platforms using LibGDX.

2. Learn about the key features of LibGDX that will ease and speed up your development cycles.

3. An easy-to-follow, comprehensive guide that will help you develop games in LibGDX successfully.

LibGDX Game Development Essentials

ISBN: 978-1-78439-929-0   Paperback: 216 pages

Make the most of game development features powered by LibGDX and create a side-scrolling action game, Thrust Copter

1. Utilize the robust features of LibGDX to easily create and publish cross-platform 2D and 3D games that involve complicated physics

2. Be the best cross-platform game developer with the ability to create rich interactive applications on all the leading platforms

3. Develop a 2D side scrolling game, Thrust Copter, add physics, and try to convert it to 3D while working on interesting LibGDX experiments

Please check **www.PacktPub.com** for information on our titles

Libgdx Cross-platform Game Development Cookbook

ISBN: 978-1-78328-729-1   Paperback: 516 pages

Over 75 practical recipes to help you master cross-platform 2D game development using the powerful Libgdx framework

1. Gain an in-depth understanding of every Libgdx subsystem, including 2D graphics, input, audio, file extensions, and third-party libraries.

2. Write once and deploy to Windows, Linux, Mac, Android, iOS, and browsers.

3. Full of uniquely structured recipes that help you get the most out of Libgdx.

Learning Libgdx Game Development

ISBN: 978-1-78216-604-7   Paperback: 388 pages

Walk through a complete game development cycle with practical examples and build cross-platform games with Libgdx

1. Create a LibGDX multi-platform game from start to finish.

2. Learn about the key features of LibGDX that will ease and speed up your development cycles.

3. Write your game code once and run it on a multitude of platforms using LibGDX.

Please check **www.PacktPub.com** for information on our titles